The Spanish Mousetrap is the story of how a queen's infatuation, a king's weakness and a prince's vindictiveness led Napoleon to believe that he could dispose of Spain as he wished in order to clear the way for his conquest of England. It tells how Napoleon lured his victims to a carefully prepared ambush at Bayonne where, in May 1808, he forced the Spanish king and his heir to abdicate. It took him eight years to achieve this aim — which led in its turn to the Peninsular War and ultimately to Napoleon's own downfall.

Nina Epton reveals the human passions and intrigues seething in and around the Spanish court, and the whole bizarre tale is recounted in vivid and dramatic narrative, often in words attributed to the characters themselves. In her reconstruction of what Napoleon himself called this 'drama in five acts', the author draws on Napoleon's letters and the memoirs of eye-witnesses in French and Spanish. Among the illustrations in *The Spanish Mousetrap* are portraits by Goya, who painted most of the extraordinary protagonists with cruelly candid realism.

Nina Epton writes about Maria Luisa, the passionate Queen of Spain, and her husband, Charles IV, who turned a blind eye to what went on behind his back. Their son, Prince Ferdinand of Asturias — at one time accused of wishing to murder his parents and imprisoned in the gloomy Escorial — nursed a Hamlet-like hatred of his mother and her alleged lover, the all-powerful Manuel Godoy. It was Ferdinand and his partisans who overthrew Godoy — but constantly looming in the background was the despotic figure of Napoleon, forever asking Spain for more money, soldiers, ships to assist him in his designs . . .

THE SPANISH MOUSETRAP

Nina Epton

THE SPANISH MOUSETRAP

Napoleon and the Court of Spain

Macdonald · London

For Rocío Arnáez

First published in Great Britain in 1973
by Macdonald and Company (Publishers) Limited
49/50 Poland Street, London W.1

Printed in Great Britain by
Redwood Press Limited, Trowbridge, Wiltshire

CONTENTS

ILLUSTRATIONS

All the portraits are by Goya, and are reproduced by courtesy of the Prado Museum in Madrid, with the exception of that of Pepita Tudó (from the miniature by V. López) which was photographed for this book by the Prado Museum photographer, Sr. Manso, from the Colección Lazaro Galdeano, Madrid. The pictures of the royal palaces are by courtesy of the Dirección General del Turismo, Madrid.

PART ONE

THE COURT AND SOCIETY:
THE PALACE TRIANGLE

I

The carriage bearing Monsieur Alquier, the recently appointed French ambassador to the court of Their Spanish Majesties Charles IV and Maria Luisa, rumbled along the rain-furrowed road from the Spanish frontier town of Irún on its devious way to Madrid.

It was the end of November in the last year of the eighteenth century but it could have been the first as far as Spain was concerned, Monsieur Alquier reflected as he peered at the tight-lipped Basques in their shaggy sheepskin jackets and their archaic farm implements. He had been warned that Spanish inns were atrocious so he had brought his own provisions. He felt as if he had been transported in time to the remotest regions of pre-revolutionary France. Yet the scattered Basque farms were well kept and their owners looked prosperous compared to those of treeless Castile; there icy winds swept through villages huddled round churches like chicks under a hen's wing in the middle of wheat-producing plains, two-thirds of which belonged to the clergy and the nobility.

How ill-clad the peasants were, how sombre and haughty they looked! Many of the cheerless stone houses proudly displayed carved escutcheons over doorways leading to dung-filled courtyards. In the towns, the plazas were filled with a bizarre assortment of beggers, retainers and hangers-on attracted by aristocratic waste and church alms. The Spanish empire stretched from California to the Straits of Magellan, but there were few visible signs of wealth in the mother country. The aristocrats lived uncomfortably and there were no ostentatious princes of the church such as one found in Italy.

Monsieur Alquier made careful notes of all he saw as he had been instructed by his masters — the leaders of the Directoire — and, above all, by General Bonaparte, who was now beginning to take a more active interest in this hispanic continent so awkwardly situated (for his purpose) between his arch-enemy England and the eastern Mediterranean which he dreamed of conquering.

The new ambassador was deliberately taking a zigzag route so that he could visit the northern ports and make useful contacts who would report to him regularly on the activities of Pasajes, San Sebastian, Bilbao, El Ferrol, Corunna. It displeased him to see British ships loading and discharging cargoes in nearly all of these ports. A brisk trade was evidently going on between England and Spain. This would have to be stopped.

In the inland university towns of Santiago de Compostela, Salamanca, Valladolid, Monsieur Alquier found a general indifference to learning and the academics engaged in double employment to earn a living.

Throughout his journey his modern carriage and smart equipage were greatly admired; even the citizens of Madrid were surprised by such a display of elegance from the new Republic, and when the ambassador was presented at court he pleased The Kings (as Charles IV and Maria Luisa were jointly called) by his urbane manners. They had expected a rougher type of representative from the new regime. So not all men of polish and refinement had been swept away by the Terror, with their unfortunate cousin Louis XVI and his queen, Marie-Antoinette! (Charles had sent an appeal to the *Constituante* to spare Louis, but it had been couched in such unrealistic, domineering terms that it had not been taken seriously. The French leaders were well aware that the Spanish King was powerless and they resented his interference.)

Monsieur Alquier was far less impressed by Charles and Maria Luisa than they were by him. He began to convey his impressions to General Bonaparte in a flow of vivid, gossipy dispatches.

Charles IV, he reported, bore a distinct physical resemblance to Louis XVI with his long Bourbon nose and upturned chin. Born in Italy, his father Charles III had kept him away from public affairs. There was a streak of insanity in the family and Charles III had advocated fresh air and exercise for his son, fearing to overtax his brain; but there was not much brain to be overtaxed. (Charles III had made many improvements in Spain's outdated administration and economy but these were abandoned when his son succeeded him in 1788.) Alquier wrote that:

> The King has no idea how to govern and no particular desire to do so. His main interests are hunting, tinkering with clocks and watches [a penchant shared by many Bourbons] and leatherwork. In the evenings he plays cards with two or three old gentlemen attached to the court like barnacles to a rock, or plays the violin very fast and very badly.
>
> His people like and respect him. For one thing, he looks kingly and appearance counts for much in Spain. He is tall, dignified and benign; he is known to be a good husband, he has no mistresses, he is pious and he speaks in the same easy terms to high and low alike, slapping both familiarly and often quite violently on the shoulder.

Monsieur Alquier also reported the current rumour that the King's doctors had advised him not to visit his wife's bedchamber too often and that the King had not found this injunction displeasing, thus insinuating that the sovereign was, to use a modern idiom, undersexed.

Maria Luisa was forty-nine years old, three years older than her husband, and his first cousin. She was dark, prematurely toothless (so she took her meals alone), olive-skinned and ugly, but she moved gracefully and was more articulate than her consort. Her best feature, prominently displayed in all her pictures, were her plump white arms. Her tutor in Italy – she was born in Parma – had been the philosopher Condillac, but as the Princess was married at the early age of thirteen and a half, she had had little time in which to be imbued with philosophical theories. She was alleged to be hot-blooded and passionate. Scandalous stories of her amours with young guardsmen had been recounted and repeated in most European courts by amused observers, few of them closely connected with the palace. The person nearest to the Queen, the King, was the only one who seemed to be unaware of his wife's lustfulness. Since he was personally responsible (one assumes) for her twenty-four childbirths and miscarriages, it is difficult to believe that the Queen had much leisure for dalliance.

Since 1792, however, her name had been linked with that of a former guardsman, thirty-seven-year-old Manuel Godoy, descended from a minor noble family of Estremadura, a province bordering on Portugal, known for pig-rearing and the extreme poverty of its inhabitants. Godoy's enemies (they ranged from church dignitaries to grandees) nicknamed him 'the sausage merchant'. The Kings had bestowed upon him the novel title of 'Prince of the Peace' in 1795 in return for the part he had played in bringing about the Treaty of Bale with France. This was the latest, but not the last, of a string of titles which he had collected in such a short period of time, for apparently no good reason, that tongues were bound to wag.

Spanish nobles were particularly shocked when, in 1797, Manuel Godoy, Duke of Alcudia, Prince of the Peace, First Secretary of State, possessor of the Order of the Golden Fleece, and the Queen's private secretary, was married to Maria Teresa of Bourbon and Villabriga, Countess of Chinchón, the King's cousin, daughter of Charles's uncle Louis, who had contracted a morganatic marriage and lived in seclusion in Toledo. By this marriage, Godoy became related to the royal family and entitled to wear royal livery. Gossips said that the marriage had been arranged by the Queen in a supreme effort to detach the favourite from Pepita Tudó, the only one of his many mistresses to whom he was sincerely attached.

Pepita had apparently entered his life the way so many other women had, in the role of a petitioner. She had come from the provinces with her mother to ask Godoy to intervene in a village land dispute. Pepita's widowed mother was being abused by the local authorities because she was poor and defenceless. They had heard that the Prince of the Peace often took up just causes and protected people like them when he could spare the time from his many duties, so they had made the arduous journey to Madrid by canvas-covered barrel cart, hoping against hope. Godoy was moved – not by their story, which was commonplace, but by Pepita's good looks. It was common knowledge that he was susceptible to women, that behind his office was a cosy recess furnished with a divan where, once a bargain had been struck with a fair petitioner, she could pay him back immediately in feminine currency. Many parents and guardians accepted the position with a complaisance that roused the fiery preacher Fray Diego of Cadiz to paroxysms of holy wrath.

When Pepita became Godoy's mistress she thoughtfully provided for her mother who had started her on her career. (Godoy married her in 1828 after his wife's death. In the meantime, Pepita had been lady-in-waiting to the Queen for years and had received the title of Countess of Castel Fiel. The virtuous King appears to have been blind to this infatuation too.)

After his marriage to the King's cousin, Godoy pocketed his dowry of five million reales and set up Pepita Tudó in a handsome residence close to his own. The Queen, or so it was rumoured, went back out of pique to one of the royal bodyguards, Mallo, and lent an ear to Godoy's rivals. At the time of Monsieur Alquier's arrival in the capital, Godoy had been in disgrace for nearly a year. Foreign relations were in the hands of the volatile Voltairian Señor Urquijo.

The new ambassador had little to report to Paris about the heir to the throne, sixteen-year-old Prince Ferdinand, who kept to his apartments and lived in fear of his parents who were always scolding him. From a sickly child he had grown into an awkward, sullen adolescent who found servants congenial company. Very probably they had enlightened him on the subject of his mother's relations with Godoy to whom he had taken such a violent dislike that his royal parents were pained. How could anyone *not* like their dear Manuel? For Charles too was deeply fond of Godoy. The true nature of his feelings towards the favourite must be left to psychoanalytical conjecture.

Monsieur Alquier, however, did not conjecture. He believed, like everybody else, that the King's virtue and indolence explained his blindness to the Queen's supposed infidelities and his weakness for Godoy who, even during his period of disgrace, continued to appear at court.

Court life was so formal and tedious that the French ambassador could easily understand why an ardent woman like Maria Luisa sought to escape from it. The pomp and rigidity of the ceremonial reminded him of the seventeenth century. The royal calendar, set in motion by Charles III, never varied: on 7 or 8 October the court left the palace of San Ildefonso near Segovia north of Madrid for that of the Escorial, or San Lorenzo; they returned to Madrid until the Wednesday after Easter and then left for Aranjuez, an oasis on the banks of the Tagus, fifty miles south of the capital, until the end of June. A fortnight was spent in Madrid before further visits to the Escorial and San Ildefonso. 'An expensive year,' remarked Monsieur Alquier, 'which costs The Kings 105 million reales – nearly a third of the national revenue.'

Unlike Paris, there were few monuments of architectural interest in Madrid, which had only become the capital of Spain in the seventeenth century and been neglected by its monarchs. The 'sights' were essentially mobile and human, from the *majos* of the poor quarters to the daily parade of grandees in their carriages in the Prado, that wide tree-lined avenue still unequalled in Europe. The most extraordinary scene of all in the Prado was at the time of the Angelus, announced by the city's many church bells at 6 p.m., when the carriages suddenly stopped and their occupants fell silent while the ladies fingered their rosaries. Even the horses appeared to understand that they too should remain still – as if a magic spell had been cast upon them.

On the whole, Madrid's high society was as stiff as the high-backed chairs upon which Spanish ladies sat and fanned themselves in houses which were bitterly cold in winter and heated only by small braziers. One of the first things

Monsieur Alquier did was to have a chimney built in his residence but then he found that wood was scarce – and coal was hardly ever used.

Few aristocratic ladies (or gentlemen) were cultured; many ladies were attended by slave-like lovers; they were usually very dull, with a few notable exceptions. The most notable was the notorious Duchess of Alba-Cayetana, whom the proud court painter Goya followed like one of the Duchess's poodles – a dangerous pursuit, for she was young, gay, an inconsequential female Doña Juana, whereas Goya was fifty and rapidly becoming deaf.

The Duchess belonged to the coterie of younger generation aristocrats who, having no culture of their own (the little they had was derived from France and they were known as 'the Frenchified'), found more pleasure in the company of Madrid's dancing, singing and bullfight-loving lower classes than in the dreary drawing-rooms of their peers. It was fashionable to ape the dress and manners of the *majos* and *majas* of the popular Lavapies district of Madrid whom Goya immortalized in his frescoes on the life of Saint Anthony in the chapel of La Florida built on the banks of the shallow Manzanares. That was where gaiety abounded – among the people, who carried themselves with regal poise: picaresque, picturesque, warm, violent and voluble. To mix with them was an exciting, exhilarating experience; shallow, no doubt, as a passing shadow show, but never debasing. The majos of Madrid, unlike their contemporaries and social equals in other European countries of the time, possessed dignity; in addition, they had a gift for repartee and – above all – an unquenchable vitality.

Monsieur Alquier often saw Cayetana, Duchess of Alba, at bullfights in the company of Goya. She was not beautiful in the classical sense but her pert, provocative attractiveness had a *gamine* quality unique among the rigid Spanish beauties of the day. Her small features and pale oval face set in a mass of shoulder length black hair came to life when she laughed, and she often laughed, disclosing small pearly teeth. Goya never painted her in these gay moods, but with her firm lips tightly closed as though they were determined not to reveal the secret of their hold over the painter. He may have believed that by doing so she would appear more dignified to posterity, but he only succeeded in making her look like a spoiled child pausing between pranks.

One of Monsieur Alquier's many spies gave him a detailed account of the prank which caused Cayetana to be banned from court for a year. This is what the spy, who appears to have been singularly ubiquitous and omniscient, related to the gullible ambassador.

The Duchess had been to visit Goya in his studio, as she often did, accompanied by her faithful dwarf Bonito. The artist allowed few people to visit him in his hide-out; he preferred to work in solitude, but he made an exception for the stimulating Cayetana. Her childish gaiety restored his spirits which, since his growing deafness, were becoming more and more melancholy.

The Duchess had brought a box of cosmetics with her, containing powders, rouge and kohl, which she emptied on to a table near the easel. She was tired of them, she told Goya, and she wanted him to try a novel experiment by painting her face as if he were working on a canvas. How long would it take him? He would have to paint quickly, she commanded, because she wanted to look particularly radiant that evening.

Goya probably thought that Cayetana was planning to appear at a fancy-dress ball and he agreed to her unusual request, only putting down his brushes when she calmly informed him that she intended to drive in the Prado that afternoon and to cause a sensation.

At first he could not believe her. Moreover, he had qualms about the possible effect of the oil paint upon her delicate complexion; but Cayetana urged him to proceed. From time to time she looked at herself in a pocket mirror and nodded with pleasure.

Could it be true that she was going to parade in the Prado

and take her place among the carriages of the other grandees, painted like a trollop?

Cayetana confided her plan; it was the culmination of a premeditated revenge on the Queen who, she assured Goya, was jealous of her looks and popularity and had tried to have her Madrid palace burnt down on two occasions. Goya could hardly believe this apparently wild story but Cayetana was sure – her servants, who had friends at the royal palace, had assured her that it was true. The Queen, to whom Cayetana referred in highly disrespectful terms, bore her a personal grudge and she would stop at nothing because she was a vindictive Italian. No doubt the Queen would have liked to separate the artist from his muse and favourite model, but Goya's position was too secure; he had been appointed court painter during the reign of Charles II and furthermore he was one of Godoy's protégés.

Cayetana informed Goya that she had sent two of her maids to Paris as spies on a very feminine mission, for she was not in the least interested in politics. Her spies were sharp-eyed needlewomen who had been instructed by their mischievous mistress to call upon the fashionable dressmaker, Mademoiselle Minette, and to wheedle their way into her workshop in the guise of embroideresses. They were excellent workers and so their task was easy. Goya had presumably never heard of Mademoiselle Minette, a clever little woman who made dresses for the wealthy wives and mistresses of the Directoire leaders, including General Bonaparte's consort Josephine ex-Beauharnais, and from whom Maria Luisa had ordered a gala dress. This had been reported to the Duchess by her private network of informers.

Cayetana's maids took careful notes and later made an exact copy of the dress which Maria Luisa was going to wear that very night at a palace reception. Cayetana's outrageous scheme was to dress herself in plain black with a black lace mantilla in the *maja* style which even the Queen had copied for one of her portraits by Goya, and to drive through the Prado in an open carriage flanked by her maid who would be

attired in the orange satin 'creation' ordered by the Queen
from Mademoiselle Minette (Maria Luisa had a predilection
for orange and yellow although these colours did not suit her
sallow complexion, which large patches of rouge on her
cheeks could not entirely efface).

The contrast between the Duchess of Alba in her black
maja outfit and her maid in orange would be bound to attract
attention and then, later in the day, when the dress was seen
on the Queen – why, it would set the whole of Madrid
rocking with mirth!

Monsieur Alquier's spy had been told that Cayetana would
have liked Goya to accompany her on the drive but this he
firmly refused to do, out of loyalty to his royal patrons. The
Duchess fumed and pouted, but her lover was adamant. He
was growing old and too solemn for such practical jokes.

Cayetana was as good as her word. Her prank was the talk
of Madrid. More than that, it was almost responsible for a
diplomatic incident. Maria Luisa was furious when she heard
that the Duchess of Alba had been seen wearing a copy of her
gala dress that afternoon. How dare Mademoiselle Minette be
so careless – how could she have shown the model to
strangers? Monsieur Alquier was informed and he felt obliged
to apologize on behalf of the fashionable Parisian dressmaker
and to make amends by promising that a new toilette would
be sent to the irate Queen from Paris as a gift. He went so far
as to hint that he would ask for the dress to be selected by no
less discriminating a person than Josephine Bonaparte herself.

The Queen was mollified. She was vastly intrigued by the
stories she had heard of Bonaparte's infatuation for the
elegant creole who accompanied her husband on his campaigns and whose bedroom was said to be decorated in
military style with an enormous bed in the shape of a tent.
Josephine was reputed to have an exquisite and daring taste
in clothes: she wore clinging white dresses to reveal her
shapely curves and did not need a corset. In the eyes of Maria
Luisa it was of course unfortunate that Josephine was tied to
Bonaparte by a civil marriage only – invalid in the eyes of

the church. Still, a civil marriage was better than no marriage at all and it was reported that Bonaparte frowned on free love as it had been practised by the first revolutionary leaders and still by some members of his entourage – notably his Foreign Minister Monsieur de Talleyrand, who was devoted to his very ordinary-looking mistress, Madame Grand.

Charles Maurice de Talleyrand-Perigord, ex-Bishop of Autun, whose nurse had accidentally dropped him when he was an infant, hence his limp, came of an old aristocratic French family. In his youth he had attended the coronation of Louis XVI, a sovereign whom he quickly forgot so as to be able to serve the new revolutionary masters. Now he was temporarily devoted to Bonaparte, whose star was in the ascendant, for as long as it suited his purpose and his insatiable pockets. Monsieur de Talleyrand had expensive and aesthetic tastes.

Despite his lameness, his retroussé nose, his insolent haughtiness, he was much sought after by the ladies for his wit and indolent charm. Men, Bonaparte in particular, admired his brilliant mind and diplomatic gifts.

II

When General Bonaparte received Monsieur Alquier's dispatch he must have smiled ironically as he came to the following passage: 'We could perhaps pacify the Queen by sending her a couple of dresses, something suitable for a piquant brunette of twenty.' As Monsieur Alquier had hoped, Bonaparte called Josephine to his aid for this feminine assignment. As for Charles, Monsieur Alquier went on, he would be delighted to receive two guns of French manufacture – so he had intimated to the ambassador.

It did not displease Bonaparte to learn that French products were so keenly appreciated by the Spanish court. France was very much alone and he needed friends and allies.

He called for Monsieur de Talleyrand and showed him the latest gazette from Madrid.

Monsieur de Talleyrand always took his time. Unlike Bonaparte he was never in a hurry. He retained the graceful manners and the habits of a courtier of the old regime, delicately and frequently helping himself to a pinch of snuff from a gold enamelled snuffbox.

'Alquier is the most readable as well as the most futile of our ambassadors,' he commented.

'If we are to deal seriously with Spain he will have to be replaced,' Bonaparte replied. 'His Most Catholic Majesty can be useful to us, thanks to his good relations with Rome. It would not suit our purpose to have an Austrian elected to the papacy by the Conclave, as is planned. An Italian, approved by Spain, would be more pliable and favourable to our negotiations for a Concordat.'

Monsieur de Talleyrand could not but agree, since he had already put the idea into Bonaparte's head.

'The Grand Duchy of Parma,' Bonaparte continued, 'is now in the possession of Ferdinand, Maria Luisa's brother. I should prefer to see him and his heirs pushed gently towards the periphery, to a new kingdom which could be carved out of Tuscany. This would leave us within striking distance of Austria. It would be pointed out to Their Catholic Majesties that this kingdom, with a few territorial additions, would be larger than Tuscany. I suggest it could be called Etruria.'

Talleyrand observed that the Grand Duke Ferdinand might not agree but he added: 'His state of health is precarious so let us hope that his Maker will arrange things for us opportunely. On the other hand, since it is believed that the Spanish Kings intend to marry their daughter Maria Luisa to Ferdinand's son Louis, they would no doubt be pleased to have the couple well provided for. They do not appear to manage their financial affairs very well.'

The Spanish treasury was another subject of the greatest interest to Bonaparte, who was under the impression that the silver pouring into Spain from her South American colonies was a ceaseless horn of plenty. French finances were at a low ebb. Furthermore, the English fleet was an obstacle to the smooth transfer of silver from America to Europe and Bonaparte wanted the Spanish fleet to assist him in his campaign against England in the colonies. The French naval division in the Rio de la Plata was in urgent need of reinforcements, and four more expeditions were being planned.

In exchange for the new kingdom to be created in Italy for the Spanish Bourbons, Bonaparte intended to ask Spain for Louisiana, a territory which would serve as a springboard for French operations against San Domingo and the English.

Last but by no means least there was Portugal to admonish and prevent from helping the English by giving protection to their ships. Spanish intervention would be useful there too.

Bonaparte and Talleyrand agreed that Monsieur Alquier was incapable of conducting such delicate negotiations and they decided to replace him by the much tougher General Berthier.

Monsieur Alquier's ambassadorship in Spain lasted barely three months. He left Madrid on 20 February 1800, for Florence, and General Berthier replaced him in March. Much had happened in Madrid in the interval. For one thing, Manuel Godoy had been restored to complete favour, this time for good.

III

What could have made Godoy so attractive to The Kings? He was not handsome. Goya painted several portraits of him and he can be relied upon for fidelity to the point of cruelty. Godoy was of medium height, and inclined to obesity; his complexion was fair, his face heavy, with a sensual mouth and the lazy expression of a pampered Señorito. He was indeed the pampered darling of the doting sovereigns and in all his portraits he looks out upon the world with a self-assured air and a lazy smile. There is no trace of arrogance in his expression or stance, no more than a schoolboyish pose even when he is portrayed as a conquering hero in a splendid uniform upon a fiery steed which one cannot take seriously, for it looks so much like what it really was: a game of make-believe.

Godoy's enemies accused him of womanizing, corruption, ambition, but the same could be (and was currently) said of other politicians of his time elsewhere. He was no sanguinary tyrant; he banished his rivals, true, but he did not have them poisoned or executed. The historian Raymond Carr has described him, politically, as 'a mild progressive'. He invited the leading intellectuals to his receptions and founded several educational institutions. He took an interest in botany, in welfare schemes for foundlings, and in the teaching of the deaf. (He learned sign language himself so as to be able to communicate with his friend Goya.) Foreigners commented on his graciousness, his bonhomie, his easy manners and his generosity. During hostilities with England he not only released a young English volunteer in the colonies, he allowed his father a free passage to the Indies to release him in person, with a warrant from the favourite, upon the recommendation of Lord Holland, who had met and liked Godoy. But all that still does not quite explain why Charles and Maria Luisa became so attached to Godoy that they were said – in France – to form 'an inseparable Trinity'.

Godoy's charm, his nonchalance, seem to have acted like a magnet upon The Kings whether or not – and it will probably never be proved – he was at one time the Queen's lover. It is obvious that he succeeded in drawing out the maternal and paternal instincts of his royal patrons. They loved him, as subsequent events will show, more than their own flesh and blood, more than their life, more than their throne.

The King could not bear to be parted from his 'dear Manuel' any more than the Queen could. The three of them formed a strangely assorted and ambiguous trio. A strong element of Godoy's success may be explained by his gay, open character in contrast to the formality of the courtiers and aristocrats who gyrated round The Kings. In the many letters to Godoy which have survived, Maria Luisa frequently refers to his gaiety and his happy nature. He seems to have been the only amusing person in the royal circle and, in addition, unassuming and unservile. The Kings' fatal mistake was to believe that dear Manuel was brilliantly clever, which he was not; and they trusted in his political acumen implicitly. It was their misfortune that he should have had to pit his wits against a man of Bonaparte's stature. From his ostentatious mansion of Buenavista close to the royal palace, Godoy crossed daily to the King's study on the first floor to discuss affairs of state with the Queen. Papers for the King's signature were submitted to him upon his return from the chase.

Charles rose punctually at 5 a.m. A little before that hour, every morning, lights began to appear in the royal palace. This palace, rebuilt by the first Bourbon King, Philip V, grandson of Louis XIV, lies on the north-east edge of the city over-looking the hunting grounds of the Casa del Campo and the distant sierra of Guadarrama. It stands aloof and apart from the city's inhabitants, in cold isolation. Gusts of wind came howling from the sierra in the winter like packs of famished wolves. They seemed to blow from the same direction until they hurled themselves upon the palace walls, when they divided into separate destructive entities; some swept across the courtyards to beat upon the heavy doors of the royal armoury, others shook at those of the stables, while the smaller ones pushed through the chinks in the sentries' boxes. Many sentries were frostbitten and some even froze to death during a particularly severe spell.

More lights flickered in the kitchens where the servants prepared the King's substantial breakfast, and in the heavy, gilded Baroque chapel in the centre of the palace where cherubs smiled coyly above the heads of the priest and his acolytes as they made ready for their sovereign to hear his first Mass of the day.

A little later, muffled figures began to run to and fro between the stables, carriage wheels resounded on the cobblestones, horses neighed and stamped, grooms swore under their vaporous breath as the hunting cavalcade formed and drew up in front of the palace gates. This programme never varied, winter or summer: the Captain of the Guard rode in the first carriage with the Master of the Horse, the Chief Equerry and a Gentleman of the Chamber; the King sat in the second carriage, followed by an empty one in case of a breakdown; the third carriage was filled with the noblemen invited to the royal hunt, the fourth was occupied by the surgeon and physician, the fifth carried the Captain of the Hunt, a gunsmith and the King's hunting clothes. The royal hunt occupied two hundred and fifty people every day and on special occasions, involving an extra heavy slaughter of animals, the number rose to two thousand.

Godoy stayed with the Queen for a couple of hours every morning and then she would go down to watch him mount for his daily ride in the Casa del Campo. It is not to be wondered that the Prince of Asturias resented the favourite and felt that he was screening him from his parents' affection. In January 1800, the Prince had more reason than ever to detest Godoy who had persuaded The Kings to relieve his beloved tutor, Canon Escoiquiz, of his duties and to give him a post as archdeacon in Toledo.

This tall, gaunt Navarrese, who was to play such an important role in the events that led to the abdication at Bayonne, had been appointed tutor to Ferdinand in 1796 by Godoy himself, as a person whom he believed he could trust to spy upon the Prince's attitudes and activities. There were a number of aristocrats at court who hated the favourite and were ready to side with the Prince against him. They needed to be watched.

Escoiquiz, however, befriended the neglected Prince and gained his confidence. When Godoy fell from favour in 1798, he had the temerity to present the Queen with a long essay on how the kingdom should be governed which contained transparent allusions to the weaknesses of the Prince of the Peace. In his Memoirs, Escoiquiz takes pains to assure his readers that Maria Luisa encouraged him to write this essay which she put away and later showed to Godoy – hence the reason for his subsequent dismissal.

The Canon was proud of his literary leanings. He had translated Milton's *Paradise Lost* and Young's *Elegy* into Spanish and composed a tedious poem on the Conquest of Mexico in which he extolled Charles and Maria Luisa. He did not stimulate a love of books in his royal pupil who was more interested in the bindings than the contents, but then he could not have had time to teach the Prince much during his one hour's daily lesson which, according to the terms of his contract, was to consist of mathematics and geography. Other tutors taught Ferdinand and his brother Carlos music, dancing, fencing and the military arts. The Canon's suggestion that the heir to the throne be allowed to assist at royal councils was peremptorily dismissed. Charles III had never allowed his son to do so and it was not considered advisable to burden the Prince's brain. He saw little of his parents, and more of his eccentric little uncle, Don Antonio, the King's wizened brother, with whom the Prince played billiards, draughts and card games.

Sometimes Ferdinand walked through the royal parks with his valets and distributed alms to the needy who approached him through the railings. People felt intuitively that the Prince was unloved and relegated to the background. He was a shadowy figure about whom little was known, but he was the heir to the throne and as such sacred in their eyes. The aura of mystery enhanced him in the public eye and he was applauded on the infrequent occasions he was seen riding in a carriage behind his parents. Years later, the Spanish people discovered that Ferdinand, the 'Desired One' as they called him during his exile in France, had inherited the worst traits of his mother in addition to defects caused by his faulty upbringing: malevolence, vindictiveness, cruelty, cunning and indecisiveness.

After Canon Escoiquiz was banished Ferdinand continued to exchange letters with him through his footmen. Godoy, in his memoirs, writes that he made efforts to gain Ferdinand's friendship but that it proved impossible. This does not sound convincing. One cannot help feeling that the favourite simply did not believe it was worth his while to cultivate the boorish Prince whose jealousy was insurmountable.

IV

When the news of Bonaparte's victory over the Austrians at Marengo in June 1800 reached Spain, Charles was full of praise for his brilliant ally. 'What a splendid strategist he is — what a remarkable man!' he cried, adding primly, 'And he is as good a Catholic as I am.' (Bonaparte had been careful to arrange for Charles's equerries to hear Mass when they escorted his gift of sixteen Andalusian horses for the General across France. Such details impressed the King.)

They thought the moment opportune to discuss the affairs of their daughter Maria Luisa. Could General Bonaparte not find a way of extending her husband Louis' dominions in Italy? And so it was that Charles himself broached the subject of the negotiations which Bonaparte was so eager to enter into.

General Berthier was called to San Ildefonso by The Kings for the preliminary negotiations of the treaty with France, but first he had to attend the feast of St Louis which was celebrated every year by a royal garden fête and a display of the splendid fountains commissioned by Elizabeth Farnese, wife of Philip V, Charles's French grandfather.

The wooded gardens of the pink and grey palace at the foot of the Guadarrama were filled with silk and satin-clad visitors. The courtiers and grandees were delighted to exchange the August heat of the capital for the shady avenues and cool greenery of this summer residence near Segovia. They were less delighted, however, to find that Charles was in one of his boisterous moods. He roared with laughter as he soused three of his unsuspecting guests with jets of water from cleverly concealed orifices near the fountain of the Three Graces. When he was in this mood, and after the departure of his guests, he would frequently go to the stables and engage in wrestling bouts with his grooms.

There was thunder in the air and Maria Luisa fingered her coral necklace apprehensively; she wore this necklace, from which dangled a score of holy relics, almost continually at San Ildefonso where there was a constant risk of summer storms from the surrounding mountains. At the first clap of thunder the Queen would order her servants to light a dozen candles to St Barbara in the chapel and in her private apartments. The superstitious Queen shared the belief of her subjects that this saint had special powers to ward off storms.

When the fête was over the treaty discussions began between General Berthier and Urquijo. They dragged on throughout the summer both at San Ildefonso and at Aranjuez, a neat little white town built exclusively for the court.

The pale gold palace, rebuilt in the grand Versailles manner by Philip V, stood behind a vast forecourt framed by a wall of elms, the first to be planted in Spain. In front of the palace was a wide colonnaded plaza containing the dwellings of the members of the court. Godoy had a residence facing the gardens that bordered the Tagus, where golden pheasants roamed like living ornaments from an eastern temple. At Aranjuez the Tagus flows deep and green, fertilizing the adjacent market-gardens famous for their luscious straw-berries and asparagus. Gilded gondolas were kept in the royal boathouse and little Don Antonio, the King's brother, shot at half-tame hares on the islands in the river. Almost at the gates of the palace an immense heap of refuse was allowed to pile up and rot so that it might attract crows for Charles to shoot at; he was not too particular about the quality of his prey.

He had built himself a Spanish Trianon, the Casa del Labrador, in the centre of the riverside gardens, where the royal family assembled for breakfast. This bijou of a palace was constructed round a modest labourer's cottage, hence its name. The humble kitchen, by royal whim and command, had been left as it had been in the time of its original occupants. The small rooms were hung with crimson silk, the floors were laid with Spanish marble; curious and magnificent clocks, which the King himself wound up every day, ticked like cicadas in every corner. An impressive privy adjoined the Queen's bedchamber; the canopied mahogany throne was surrounded by elaborate gold decorations, with small drawers on each side for toilet paper and a crimson velvet footstool.

The Treaty of Aranjuez was the last document to be signed by Foreign Minister Urquijo, whom Godoy was manoeuvring to banish on the pretext, inter alia, of his anti-clerical views, and replace by his docile and mediocre cousin Don Pedro Cevallos. The Queen followed the discussions closely but the legal jargon bewildered her. 'This business is very agitating and I shall not be at peace until it is settled,' she wrote to her brother Ferdinand of Parma, who was proving recalcitrant, as Monsieur de Talleyrand had foreseen. The treaty was ratified in February 1801, two months after General Bonaparte had been appointed First Consul. On this occasion Charles sent a fulsome letter of congratulations to his 'Great and dearly loved Friend', with whom from then on he was to have such varying relations.

By the Treaty of Aranjuez the Grand Duke of Parma renounced his states in favour of his son Louis, in exchange for Salzburg and other concessions, and Louis was appointed King of a new territory to be called Etruria, as Bonaparte had wished. France got Elba and above all Louisiana. This clause was kept secret so as not to alarm the English. Spain thus gave up an empire for an obscure Italian province which would eventually be swallowed up by France.

During that summer the Princes were sent to the Escorial with their tutors in advance of their parents. As soon as they arrived they were made to write to The Kings. Their formal little notes shed a curious light upon the relationships between the royal parents and their sons. Carlos wrote affectionately:

Señora, dear Mama, I am very happy to have spent several days, which passed so quickly, in the pleasant company of yourself and papa, my brothers and my aunt. I was very sorry to have to leave you, but I comply with your wishes, which I shall always obey with pleasure. Your obedient son Carlos.

Ferdinand wrote more reservedly and with a Bourbon concern for timing:

Señor, Dear Papa, I have been very happy to be in your company and that of Mama, my brothers and aunt. We have arrived safely, in three hours less a quarter. Missing the pleasant company of Your Majesty, Your most humble son, Ferdinand.

Presumably these stiff notes were prompted by the Princes' tutors but it is noticeable that Ferdinand, unlike Carlos, makes no allusion to time having passed 'quickly' in the company of his parents.

In October, Godoy's wife gave birth to a daughter. During her pregnancy The Kings had shocked both court and people – the Spaniards being sticklers for etiquette at all levels – by having waved aside the protocol and allowed the favourite's wife to enter the palace precincts and the royal drawing-room in her sedan chair. Even louder exclamations of protest were raised when The Kings announced that they would be godparents to the infant, and they took the unprecedented step of leaving the Escorial so as to be able to assist at the christening on 13 October in Madrid. The baptismal water must have been cold, for the baby girl developed conjunctivitis a few days later. This prompted Maria Luisa to write solicitously to Godoy from the Escorial:

Friend Manuel, we are delighted to hear that mother and daughter are well but are sorry to learn about the eye trouble – the left one, no doubt, into which some water fell during the baptism.

The Kings commanded Ferdinand to write a letter of congratulations to Godoy upon the birth of his daughter; he must have attempted to back out of such an uncongenial task, for the Queen wrote to Godoy:

We shall speak to Ferdinand and make him understand how much he must esteem and appreciate you. I shall inform you of the result. Ah, how right you are when you say that he is neither like his father nor like me

— a remark which reveals that far from trying to win Ferdinand's friendship, as Godoy subsequently pretended, he only widened the breach between parents and son by stressing the latter's defects. On the other hand, one may assume that the Queen's constant extolling of her 'dear Manuel' must have exasperated the young Prince. Manuel was supposed to know everything, Manuel was incomparable and he was treated as a beloved son. The more his parents complained about his coolness, the more Ferdinand withdrew into a sullen silence. This in turn irritated his parents. 'You never say anything; you never answer when we talk to you,' the Queen constantly reproached him.

PART TWO

GODOY AND THE WAR OF THE ORANGES

V

Although the negotiations between France and Spain on the subject of Etruria were proceeding smoothly, Bonaparte was not yet satisfied. As he had confided to Monsieur de Talleyrand, he wished to attack Portugal through Spain. This would be a delicate operation because there were Bourbons on that throne too. Carlota, The Kings' eldest daughter, was married to the weakling Prince Regent John of Portugal and Brazil. Godoy would have to be relied upon to override The Kings' natural repugnance to oppose their daughter and invade their ally's country.

Bonaparte could not, however, have chosen a better moment. For some months past Godoy had been impatient to prove his mettle on a field of battle. He had sent romantic appeals to Maria Luisa asking her and Charles to allow him to show how devoted he was to them and how eager for 'personal sacrifice'. Perhaps he wished to consolidate his position after having had Urquijo banished and in view of the mounting tide of popular hostility against him.

Bonaparte entrusted the Portuguese mission to his younger brother Lucien, who was promptly dispatched to Madrid for that purpose. The news that yet another French ambassador was being replaced in so short a time caused a stir at court. Godoy confided to The Kings: 'These frequent changes are disquieting. I think that Bonaparte will have to be watched carefully.'

So when young Lucien (he was twenty-five) arrived early in December 1800 to present his credentials, all eyes were coldly fixed on him, particularly since he reached the Escorial fresh from Paris without pausing to change his travel-stained clothes. Charles was momentarily displeased by this infringement of the protocol to which he was so attached.

Lucien looked like an Italian Jew. There was a mercurial quality about him which fascinated men and women alike. As his eyes swept round the distinguished assembly and he extended cordial greetings from his brother in France and expressed his friendly interest in Spain, male prejudice began to dissipate and female hearts to melt. Bonaparte had guessed correctly that Lucien's charm would mesmerize the easily swayed Kings and their favourite. Only Ferdinand was unimpressed. 'He's a typical Frenchman,' he remarked surlily; 'he looks like a dancing master.'

At first, Godoy treated the new ambassador with studied civility and a touch of arrogance, but he was soon mollified by Lucien's assurance that 'he wished to have a long talk with the Prince of the Peace as soon as it was convenient, for he had many important subjects to discuss with him and also much to learn from him.' A flatterer himself, Godoy was the first to fall for any flattery addressed to him.

When Lucien called upon Godoy at his residence with a much appreciated gift of a suit of damascened armour from Bonaparte, Godoy was delighted. The armour appeared to him to be a symbol of his current aspirations. It was a good omen. He was also pleased when Lucien launched into hyperbolic praises of Madrid.

'I had absolutely no idea that this was such a beautiful capital, that the palace was so impressive. We are very ignorant about Spain. We have nothing in Paris to compare with the Prado. I am enchanted with it, with the vivacity of the people, the beauty of your women. In fact, I *must* have a residence in the Prado,' he told Godoy, 'I shall not be satisfied until I can establish myself there surrounded by the best that the capital has to offer. You may think I am impetuous, Your Highness — maybe I am — for we Corsicans are of Mediterranean stock like the Spaniards; but you must believe me when I assure you that I already feel completely at home.'

Would it be possible to buy a residence in the much sought-after Prado? Lucien knew that all the grandees of Spain owned palaces there, that it was the fashionable and aristocratic centre of the city, that it was the most cherished dream of every Spaniard to live in that enchanted boulevard. He was prepared to pay any price; he would, he said, give many receptions, many concerts. He gave Godoy to understand that he was sociable and prepared to spend freely.

Such traits endeared him to the favourite. Lucien was a man after his own heart. He was warmer, more of an extrovert, than any of the Frenchmen he had met until then; perhaps because, as Lucien had said, the Corsicans were more like the Spaniards in temperament.

A few days after Lucien's arrival Godoy gave a magnificent reception in his honour. Thousands of red and yellow carnations were brought for the occasion by special carriages from the south of Spain as well as exotic shrubs discovered by Spanish botanists in Chile, Brazil and Peru and acclimatized in Godoy's experimental gardens of Sanlucar de Barrameda near Cadiz. Goya's murals over the marble staircase were shown off to perfection by immense flambeaux; a double row of liveried retainers, each one bearing a torch in his raised hand, extended as far as the street and greeted each arrival with a bow, the lowest bow of all, as Godoy had instructed them, being reserved for His Excellency the French Ambassador.

Lucien must have restrained a smile when, stepping from his gilded coach, which crowds pressed round to admire, he caught sight of the fleur de lys embroidered on the favourite's livery, the fleur de lys that had once graced the arms of the French Bourbons whom his brother had supplanted and which was now such a hated emblem in France. And yet this brother of his was about to create a new kingdom for the Bourbons in Italy!

The Prince of the Peace was waiting for his guest of honour at the entrance and he graciously led him up to the first floor; there, in the mirror-filled salon reflecting the velvets, brocades, satins and diamonds of the most distinguished society in Madrid, Lucien was presented to the formal Spanish nobles whose manners appeared to him so old-worldly; with very few exceptions their French was atrocious; their accents reminded him a little of his native Corsican.

Lucien noticed too that the grandees addressed Godoy as 'Your Highness' and that they did not condescend to use the familiar 'tu' in their conversation with him which they reserved for their own exclusive set. Quick-witted Lucien sensed the tension beneath the polite reception mask.

After supper Godoy led his guests to the balcony to watch a display of fireworks. Brilliantly coloured lights rocketed into the deep blue night sky tracing arabesques, golden fountains, palm trees with graceful green fronds and, finally, the royal coat of arms with the fleur de lys. The organizer of the show was Sebastian Carrion, an expert from Valencia, a city which has always been famous for pyrotechnics.

'Delightful,' exclaimed the ladies, clapping their beringed hands.

'Carrion is very clever,' observed the menfolk guardedly. The Prince of the Peace had no need to publicize the fact that he had acquired the right to use this emblem — it was typical of a parvenu to have thought of it.

Godoy followed the fireworks with childish pleasure. 'They remind me of a battlefield,' he remarked. Lucien wondered whether he had ever witnessed a battle. As far as he knew, the favourite had never been near one.

'Ah,' Godoy went on, 'if only I had the opportunity to take part in a real battle! There is nothing I long for more ardently.'

'If you really mean what you say, Your Highness,' Lucien replied, 'I think that could be very easily arranged. My brother has ideas which would, I believe, fit in with your wishes. That project I mentioned to you the other day. . . . May we talk about it soon?'

'Indeed, indeed,' Godoy said eagerly.

The squibs crackled. At that moment Godoy forgot that he disliked the sound of a cannonade — a surprising trait in a man who aspired to become Commander-in-Chief of the royal army.

VI

With Godoy's assistance the new French ambassador was rapidly installed in a mansion off the Prado. His receptions, balls and concerts, at which the celebrated pianist Boccherini played, were the most brilliant that Madrid had known. Lucien was enjoying himself in the complaisant company of the attractive Marquesa de Santa Cruz, and becoming extremely popular. His most important targets, The Kings and Godoy, had succumbed more rapidly than he had anticipated.

At a court reception the King had come up to him with a pair of shoes in his hands. 'What do you think of these, Your Excellency?' he asked Lucien jovially. 'I know that they are your size because I was careful to find out beforehand.' As Lucien stared dumbfounded at the shoes dangling from Charles's podgy hand, Godoy stepped forward with a significant wink at his new friend. 'That is the highest favour His Majesty can bestow, Your Excellency: a pair of shoes made with his own hands.'

'I am charmed, absolutely charmed, and quite over-whelmed,' Lucien stammered, for once at a loss for words.

That evening he wrote to Bonaparte:

My dear Brother, I have everybody here in the palm of my hand. The Queen pulls down the windows of her coach to salute me when she goes driving in the Prado: this is quite unprecedented. No ambassador has been so honoured before. The King, believe it or not, has presented me with a pair of shoes which he made himself in the royal workshop. (You may imagine my surprise when, without any previous intimation, these rare objects were put into my hands by His Majesty in person. They are worthy of a museum, but not very comfortable on the feet.) Godoy, whose situation vis-à-vis everybody but The Kings is very precarious, is all for me, for us. There is nothing he would not do to please his great friend Bonaparte. The time is therefore ripe to broach the subject of the treaty which you are so anxious for me to bring about. I am seeing the Prince of the Peace about it tomorrow. He is full of military ardour. As for his knowledge of military affairs, that I think I can leave to your imagination.

Lucien explained Bonaparte's objectives to Godoy in the frankest of terms. He was now intimate enough with the favourite to realize that they were in some ways birds of a feather, particularly when it came to opportunities for lining their respective nests.

'The main object, in my brother's view,' Lucien explained to Godoy, 'is to prevent Portugal from assisting England. He desires her to break off her alliance with that country and to allow Spanish troops to occupy part of her territory. It would be desirable for Spain to send an ultimatum to Portugal summoning her to do this and stating unequivocally that in case of refusal war would be declared and a French corps of 15,000 men would come to the aid of the Spanish army and occupy the northern provinces of Portugal.' This was to be the further price for the establishment of Maria Luisa's daughter and her son-in-law Louis in Etruria.

'So,' observed Godoy, 'one daughter, Carlota, and her kingdom will be sacrificed for the other, Maria Luisa and Etruria.'

'Not at all. No harm will be done to the rulers of Portugal, if they agree to cooperate with my brother. It is not his intention to engage in a bloody war. Fireworks only, dear friend, that is all. Fireworks and make-believe!

'How do you propose to achieve that end? Their Catholic Majesties would never agree to the occupation of even a part of Portugal by French troops. It would be a betrayal of their own kith and kin of which they are incapable.'

'It need not come to that,' said Lucien blandly.

'Please explain yourself more fully, Your Excellency.'

'I shall. My brother has given me carte blanche to conduct the matter with you. The intervention of French troops is planned for the ultimate phase of the operation. I believe, however, that my brother would be satisfied if we succeed in obtaining a treaty whereby Portugal agrees to close her ports to the English, gives France a part of Guyana, grants her the most favoured nation treatment in commercial affairs in South America and a monetary indemnity, say twenty-five million reales, to be paid within fifteen months.'

'In return for . . . ?'

'In return for a guarantee assuring the integrity of all Portuguese possessions.'

'How far should we push Portugal in order to persuade her to sign such a treaty? The Spanish Kings would be averse to bloodshed.'

'I am positive that we can obtain what we want with a minimum of losses. You may assure Their Catholic Majesties of that. I give you my word that this will be a mere semblance of a war. Of course we will have – you will have – to march into Portugal and fight. A little. Only a very little, otherwise we would arouse suspicions. One can hide nothing from my beloved brother, believe me! So, between ourselves, not too much comedy, but after our first successes . . . '

'Assuming that we have successes,' muttered Godoy.

'Of course we shall! The Portuguese are totally unprepared, as you must know. *You* will have an overwhelming force and furthermore you will be assisted by experienced French officers.'

Godoy saw that his dream of military prowess was about to materialize. 'I shall lead the army myself – I shall be their Commander-in-Chief,' he declared enthusiastically.

'Of course, of course, but you will be helped by men with actual experience of warfare so that nothing goes wrong. You understand, just in case. . . '

'Very well,' Godoy agreed reluctantly.

'So, after our first successes, we rush the Portuguese delegates to our tent to conclude the peace.'

'*Our* tent? Are you coming too?'

'I mean, pardon me, *your* tent. I cannot, unfortunately, take part in the campaign, but I shall expect a rapid courier from you informing me where to meet you for the parleys, since I shall sign the treaty on behalf of France. It will have to be sent to my brother to be ratified. But in the meantime we shall have made a private deal with the Portuguese. If they agree to close their ports to the English, we shall grant them an advantageous treaty and forget about the occupation of the northern provinces. From then on all will take place between you, me and the Portuguese; this will enable us to pocket a few million for ourselves, *sub rosa*. Two such very accommodating gentlemen must be rewarded, must they not? And now, dear friend,' Lucien concluded, 'I leave the preparations to you. Pray be speedy; my brother is a very impatient man.'

'How scandalous!' exclaimed Maria Luisa when Godoy reported his conversation with the French ambassador. 'How very scandalous! That French ambassador and his millions, and to think we must not, cannot breathe a word about it!'

'A scandal is to be preferred to bloodshed,' murmured Charles. 'I think we are fortunate in being able to come to an understanding with Lucien Bonaparte. My only fear is that his brother may not be satisfied.'

'Lucien believes he will.'

'I hope he is right.'

'And no harm will come to Carlota?' the Queen asked anxiously.

'None at all. Our troops will not go as far as Lisbon. There is nothing to fear.'

'The Portuguese may not agree to our demands,' the Queen objected, 'and they may appeal to the English for help.'

'They might indeed,' Godoy agreed, 'but I should be very surprised if the English respond. They will not want to face a French corps in Portugal. They are masters on the sea but not on land.'

'When do you expect to be ready to set out?' the King asked Godoy.

The favourite sat down and drew a sheet of paper from his pocket. 'Here is the list of our requirements, sire,' he replied, handing it to the King. 'I have been urged to act quickly and

I believe that everything should be ready by the end of April or the beginning of May.'

'A very good season in which to start a war,' said the Queen. 'Neither too cold nor too hot. The oranges will be ripe when you reach your native province Estremadura.'

'I see that the first item on your list is money,' sighed the King. 'How much do you need and where do you expect to get it from?'

'For a start,' said Godoy, 'I thought of appealing to the Hebrew tradesmen of Madrid, whom I have always protected. Now it is their turn to help me. I intend to impose a levy upon them which should bring in nearly sixteen million reales.'

The Queen approved the scheme. 'That way the poor will not be taxed and there will be no complaints.'

VII

The tradesmen of the capital grudgingly turned out their pockets and made up the sixteen million reales imposed upon them by Godoy, but there was still not half enough money to provide for a well-equipped and fed army. Not even for a small one.

Bonaparte sent two of his trusted Generals, Gouvion de St Cyr and Leclerc, to command the French troops and keep Godoy straight. It was not long before St Cyr reported: 'The Spanish army has no training, no confidence in its leaders or officers. It is badly fed and badly paid. The infantry lacks clothes and is in a miserable condition. There are not enough mules or horses to haul the artillery nor are there enough gun carriers.' Leclerc was kinder: 'The Spanish army would be all right if only it were well led.'

Godoy could think and talk of nothing by strategy, the deployment of troops, the relative merits of guns and cannons. He had already cast himself in the role of a minor

Bonaparte. Following this fantasy, he suggested that it would strengthen relations between the two countries if Napoleon were to be linked by marriage with the Bourbons of Spain. The Kings agreed. The First Consul was not, in their eyes, legally married to Josephine, and Lucien, who hated his sister-in-law, proposed that Their Catholic Majesties' young daughter Maria Isabella might be a good match. To this extraordinary suggestion Bonaparte retorted, but not publicly, that 'if he was ever in the position to remarry, he would not seek to do so in a ruined house.' The subject was quietly shelved.

An ultimatum was sent to Portugal at the beginning of March 1801. The Regent was given fifteen days in which to break off relations with England and close his ports to British ships. In the event of his refusal, war would be declared and France would place 15,000 men at Spain's disposal. In Paris, Monsieur de Talleyrand tried to dissuade Bonaparte from engaging in a war with Portugal which, he believed, would only profit Godoy and press the English to seek revenge by taking over Brazil from where they could attack the Spanish colonies in America.

The Portuguese sent emissaries to Paris to plead for peace. It is likely that they were made to pay liberally for Monsieur de Talleyrand's intervention in their favour.

The Prince Regent, a stout, dark-faced little man who spent his time hunting and in the company of valets, did not want a war and he made a frantic appeal for help to England. Mr John Hookham Frere was sent out as ambassador with instructions from Foreign Minister Grenville to incite Portugal to arm and have 'a just confidence in its own situation and resources'. Sir James Pulteney was ordered to re-embark the English forces stationed in Lisbon. Grenville wrote to Frere:

In the present state of war in Europe, it is not in His Majesty's power, consistent with a due regard to the safety of his own dominions, to appropriate any part of his military forces to the assistance of Portugal.

The Prince Regent was secretly informed by his in-laws

that it would be better for him and his country to submit to Franco-Spanish demands but he rejected the ultimatum. War was duly declared on 27 March 1801.

On 3 April Godoy left Madrid in a splendid new uniform to take command of his troops. It was a mild spring day; the sky was an intense, fresh blue, the golden soil of Castile stretched invitingly towards Estremadura, and the light-hearted rabble of an army, thoughtfully provided with a generous ration of wine to infuse them with a martial spirit, cheered the novice commander good-humouredly. Some of the newly recruited soldiers, who had until then been half-starving in the streets of Madrid, were not ill-disposed towards the adventure. So they marched eagerly and many of them burst into song. Godoy galloped backwards and forwards between the straggly lines, the light of battle in his eye.

That night, seated in his large and comfortable tent, he wrote his first dispatch to the Queen:

To the devil with files of papers when I am on the point of making the enemy listen to the cannon's mouth! Never shall I be able to live in future without the presence of soldiers: the sight of them thrills me and I was born never to leave them. I cannot express to Your Majesty what pleasure swells my heart. I have but one regret: ah, how happy I should be if my sovereign were here! All is bustle, warlike agitation and rousing fanfares. And all that, Madam, intoxicates and fires the imagination. Let me never hear talk again of political intruges; never, Madam, for the love of God. And may I be sent to the ends of the earth with my troops. I never wish to leave the colours. May Your Majesty deign to allow me to serve her with the sword for no shorter time than I have hitherto served her with the pen.

Before receiving this missive the Queen had written to Manuel by special courier:

I lack patience and I cannot prevent myself from writing these lines to tell you that we are anxiously awaiting your news. I am beside myself with worry. May God assist you and give you success. We pray you may return covered with laurels and we shall all celebrate your victory together.

To this she later added a post-scriptum:

Last night Cevallos came at 11 p.m. with your letter from which I read with infinite relief that you are safe and that the troops are enthusiastic at the mere sight of you. I never doubted it. The King was asleep and I did not wish to waken him since there was no particular reason to, so I immediately asked Soler to send off a courier with money so that provisions will not be lacking, or hay and oats for the French cavalry. . . . I can just picture you, friend Manuel, so gay and happy in the midst of your troops, organizing them all. I don't know what the King will say, but I can assure you that I for my part would love to be able to go and see all that is happening, and then we could all come back together. I shall be so happy to have you back at our side. We are both convinced of your military ardour, of which we have never doubted. We need you badly, and if we believe from the bottom of our hearts that without us you cannot find complete satisfaction, nor be truly happy, it is the same with us. I enclose a letter from your wife. I wrote to her two days ago. We are all well. It has been stormy today but it soon cleared up. The King has begun to take drops because his eyes have been congested. . . . Here reigns sadness, inaction and suspense, waiting for the couriers to arrive and wondering when the hour of our glory will sound, but oh! What a risk, it makes one shudder, Manuel. It makes my mouth and throat dry to think of it. Do not expose yourself too much — do not take the field on that skittish horse of yours; find one that is quieter, I implore you. . .

Today I have started taking my usual broth, to see whether it will help. I cannot vouch for the King, because he keeps his thoughts to himself, but I know that he is no less impatient and anxious than I am to have news and letters from you. He can hide his feelings better than I can. I beg you, Manuel, send us more frequent mails for we are like souls in purgatory here. It seems to me that I can hear the cannon shots, see the smoke, the horrors of war, and finally the haughty Portuguese with his knees on the ground ceding to whatever conditions you impose upon him. I hope it will all be over soon. I was sorry to hear about the bee-sting. . .

Dear Manuel does not appear to have suffered any greater personal casualty than the bee-sting referred to by the Queen.

The comic-opera army marched on, entered Portugal at midnight on 19 May, and on the morning of the 20th attacked and took the fortified town of Elvas from where Godoy could see his family house of Estremadura in the distance among the olive and orange groves.

A romantic young soldier ran up to one of the trees, cut off two branches laden with oranges and handed them gaily to Godoy, who sent them to the Queen with his daily dispatch.

What a charming gesture — and the oranges were *good*! I want this war in which you are distinguishing yourself so splendidly to be known as the 'War of the Oranges' and so it will be referred to in the Gazette.

Thus wrote the ageing Dame to her Knight.

It proved to be one of the shortest wars in history, ending four days after it had begun. There were relatively few casualties.

Having forged ahead with 30,000 men from 20 May [Godoy proudly informed the King] Your Majesty is now master of Olivenza, Elvas and Campomayor, which towns have been summoned to capitulate. The Portuguese are shut up in their fortresses and have lost three thousand men [he was exaggerating] as against one hundred Spaniards. I would have taken them all if my army had been equipped with heavy artillery. I am delighted with my troops. I hear cheers on all sides. Never have men seen more of their leader.

The people of Spain were not in the least interested in the 'War of the Oranges', which they rightly took in the light of a joke. They were far more concerned about the death of their idol the matador Pepe Hillo who was gored by a bull in Madrid. (The Queen did not like bullfights, nor did Godoy. He tried to have them suppressed but this only made him more hated than ever.)

The Queen opened her sealed letter of 24 May to inform Godoy that Lucien had urged that the Spanish troops should proceed a little further 'so that it will not be said that it is a comedy'. In a post-scriptum she added: 'Didn't I tell you so? The King says he would like to be with you and he is very happy with all you say and have done.'

These silly, impetuous letters have been quoted at length because they throw a revealing light on the relationship between the members of 'the Trinity'. The Queen's effusions are more maternal than loverlike. She writes to Manuel as she would to a dearly-loved, spoiled son. She refers openly to his wife. She appears to regret the King's apathy but is delighted to be able to add later that he shares her feelings and would like to be with his dear Manuel on the battlefield. The King is frequently mentioned but Maria Luisa acts upon her own initiative; she does not wait for Charles to wake up to ask for his instructions but immediately arranges to send funds to Manuel for army provisions. This scene, in other contexts, must have been re-enacted upon countless occasions: Charles dozing peacefully in the background, Maria Luisa taking action upon the counsel of Manuel, the King then waking up, rubbing his eyes and approving of what had been done. . .

VIII

The court of Lisbon was anxious to sign an armistice, and as soon as news reached Godoy that General Leclerc's supporting French army had entered Spain he summoned the Portuguese delegates and Lucien Bonaparte to start negotiations in his campaign tent, as had been agreed beforehand.

It was essential for Lucien to sign the peace treaty quickly so as to be able to divide the spoils before counter instructions arrived from Bonaparte in Paris. There was no time to be lost and he flew to join his fellow conspirator at Badajoz, near the Portuguese frontier.

Godoy kept his royal masters scrupulously au fait with the unofficial discussions:

Lucien has orders to demand from the Portuguese for his government fifteen million francs and his intention is to exact thirty. On my observing to him that this was a very large sum, he reduced it to twenty-five and said to me: 'Fifteen for the government and ten for us.' I said to him in reply: 'My dear friend, if the government gets fifteen you ought to be content with five for yourself, therefore you should ask for twenty.' Then he said: 'How about you? You must take your chances by the forelock. They do not come every day. You have an income of only two million. I have made four million in one year as a Minister and I mean to use all possible means to raise this figure to twelve millions.'

Lucien was on tenterhooks because the deal depended on the invaders renouncing their intended occupation of Portugal's northern provinces; he knew very well that Bonaparte would be displeased by this suggestion which had already been forwarded to Paris. Then Godoy had a flash of inspiration.

'We could,' he suggested, 'ante-date the treaty and pretend that it had been concluded before the arrival of the courier from Paris with Bonaparte's reply.'

Lucien clapped his hand. 'My dear friend, what an excellent solution! But it depends upon the utmost secrecy being maintained between our two selves. We must make a solemn pledge never, never under any circumstances whatsoever, to reveal our entente.'

Stern instructions from Bonaparte, insisting upon the maintenance of the clause on the occupation of northern Portugal and the merger of French and Spanish forces, were sent posthaste from Paris on 28 May, but by a fortunate stroke for Lucien and Godoy the courier fell from his horse outside Merida, broke his arm, and was delayed by a day. He rode into Badajoz at midday on 8 June.

The Portuguese delegates 'had already signed the ante-dated peace treaty. Fortunately, they had raised no objections.

'Now,' Godoy exclaimed, 'we can go back home with banners flying and bands playing to reap the laurels of our victory.'

Lucien, anticipating his brother's reaction, was less enthusiastic. Godoy, still in the clouds, asked him: 'Dear Friend, will you do me a great favour? Kindly ask your brother to be gracious enough to send me his portrait. I have the greatest admiration for him and nothing would please me more.'

'I shall write to him as soon as I return to Madrid,' Lucien promised him.

'When we return to Madrid,' Godoy reflected, 'I shall ask Goya to paint my portrait in my Commander's uniform.' Later, he gave the artist detailed instructions. He was to be portrayed in open country, with a sabre at his side, his aide-de-camp before him, a captured Portuguese flag waving in the background and as many horses and troops as could be fitted into the canvas. Goya obeyed but took a subtle revenge, unnoticed by his model, by making Godoy look ridiculously smug and unwarlike. He appears to be reclining on a drawing-room sofa rather than upon a field of battle.

In Madrid his devoted sovereigns were preparing fresh honours for their hero: the newly-devised title of General-issimo was bestowed upon him and the right to countersign all royal decrees. Godoy also asked for a sword of honour.

Once again The Kings made their sons send letters of congratulation to the favourite. Ferdinand must have bitten his lips when he wrote:

Dear Manuel, I congratulate you and thank you dearly for having obtained such an advantageous peace for Papa and Mama, and for all of us. I also thank you for the model cannons which Mama tells me you have brought for me. Believe me, I am looking forward to seeing you so as to congratulate you verbally. The love, fidelity and loyalty you profess towards Their Majesties are well known and also your extreme affability towards the troops, since you have made yourself loved by them and so they obeyed you readily and enabled you to make such rapid progress. Believe in the eternal friendship of your affectionate friend, Ferdinand.

The Prince's brother Francisco was made to pen a similar effusion but he succeeded in making it sound more spontaneous and childlike, as became his younger years. (He was seven.)

Manuel of the Peace, so you have won everything: cannons and guns and you have so many oranges and flags. I hope you will send me some of everything. I see your wife every afternoon and I kiss her hands. I shall be here when you come and I shall congratulate you. I have grown a lot as I take many baths. Till you come to Madrid, Francisco.

IX

There were no rejoicings in Paris when the news of Lucien's negotiations reached his brother.

'Monsieur de Talleyrand, what do you make of this?' Bonaparte thundered, tossing him the latest dispatch from Lucien, including the Portuguese treaty. He began to pace up and down his study with his hands behind his back, frowning at the thick Aubusson carpet beneath his small feet. His face had gone pale and the quivering of his nostrils presaged one of his frequent outbursts of temper that terrified both his friends and his foes.

Monsieur de Talleyrand was one of the few people who remained imperturbable during these rages and was diplomatic enough to wait until they passed before executing the orders impetuously rapped out at white heat. When Bonaparte calmed down he would present him with a milder version of his orders for signature. They were seldom altered or queried.

As the Minister scanned the document, which he had already seen before his master, Bonaparte wheeled round impatiently.

'Well, Monsieur de Talleyrand? You do not need to mince your words. I shall not mince mine. This treaty is outrageous, positively outrageous. Lucien has ignored my most pressing instructions, he has allowed himself to be hoodwinked by that – that Prince of the Peace!' He spat out the words with derision. 'You will write to Lucien,' Bonaparte commanded in a voice shrill with anger, 'that the treaty he has just signed is contrary to my instructions, contrary to the interests of the Republic and very much in the interests of the country we wish to obstruct: England. This is one of the most resounding reverses ever experienced by the First Consul, it discredits his cabinet, it is. . .' he spluttered with rage as, turning to Monsieur de Talleyrand, he saw that placid gentleman eyeing him with a faintly smug air of superiority.

Napoleon took back the document with trembling hands and threw it on the floor. 'Not a word about the occupation of the northern provinces of Portugal. Not a word about the fusion of the Franco-Spanish troops. This is treason. Treason! I never dreamed that Lucien would let himself be wound round the little finger of a man like Godoy.'

'Nor did I. Nor do I,' said Talleyrand quietly. 'In fact, I do not believe that he has been wound round anybody's little finger. I am more inclined to believe that the boot is on the other foot.'

Monsieur de Talleyrand had good friends in Portugal. He was well informed. He was also well disposed towards the Portuguese whom he had agreed to assist as far as it was in his power to do so, in exchange for . . . a stipulated consideration.

'What are you implying?' Bonaparte asked him. He had a pretty shrewd idea that his foreign minister disposed of a wide private network of informers in many countries.

'It is just possible that there may have been collusion between the two parties . . . a private agreement in the personal interests of both,' Talleyrand insinuated.

Bonaparte stared at him, thunderstruck. 'Go on,' he commanded tersely.

'Our courier arrived too late, or so it seems.'

'The courier broke his arm, he was delayed – that much has been ascertained.'

'I do not deny it. But why the hurry to sign the treaty before he arrived at Badajoz? That was unnecessary. It was known that instructions were on their way from you. I am afraid, sire, it pains me to have to say so, but – '

Bonaparte stiffened. What had Lucien been up to? Monsieur de Talleyrand was not a rumour-monger. He only spoke when he was sure of his facts.

'A little present may have been given to your brother in exchange for his signature on the ante-dated treaty,' Talleyrand suggested.

Bonaparte exploded in invectives. 'The rascal – the wretch – I shall have him recalled. Is that why he wants me to ratify the treaty at once, so that he may put a few million francs into his pockets? I shall not sign until I have obtained further concessions from Portugal. I shall *not*.'

'My information is of a highly confidential nature,' Talleyrand pointed out. 'I cannot betray my source. We shall have to act as if we were not aware of the true nature of the circumstances.'

'I don't care. I want Lucien to realize that I do know. He cannot be allowed to get away with such an enormity. I must show him that I am not to be fooled,' Bonaparte shouted.

Monsieur de Talleyrand held his peace. He had already made up his mind. He was certainly not going to allow Bonaparte to show his hand so obviously. He would of course inform Lucien on his behalf of Bonaparte's displeasure and disappointment, but without inferring that he guessed what had passed between him, Godoy and the Portuguese. In the meantime, other tactics would have to be adopted to rectify the situation.

'It might be possible to conclude a temporary peace with England,' he advanced tentatively, 'so as to free yourself on that side while you pursue your Italian campaign.'

'The English want war.'

'Not at the moment. It would be amusing if we could induce England to sign a peace treaty in which we could, indirectly, take our revenge on Spain – that is, Godoy.'

'Meaning?'

'Meaning, we could insert a clause to the effect that Trinidad would be ceded to the English. The Spaniards could do nothing about this possession of theirs, but it would irk them.'

'Bah! Trinidad is a bagatelle,' muttered Bonaparte, stooping to pick up the paper he had thrown on the floor. His temper returned as he looked at it again. 'Lucien has the impertinence to ask me to send my portrait to the Prince of the Peace! I shall never send my portrait to a man who keeps his predecessor in prison and employs the methods of the Inquisition. I may make use of him, but I despise him. You can say that when you write to Lucien.'

'You mean Señor Urquijo, Godoy's former rival? I understand that he is incarcerated in the fortress of Pamplona. Spanish Ministers of Foreign Affairs are an unfortunate breed. Saavedra and Jovellanos were likewise removed and banished by Their Majesties. I do not personally have much sympathy for Urquijo, however. In my view he is ignorant, rash and presumptuous, averse to every institution in his country and every aspiration of the people he was called upon to govern. His fanatic hostility to the Church of Rome was bound, sooner or later, to land him into serious trouble.'

'He is an anti-clerical and an admirer of Voltaire. I only wish there were more like him in Spain,' Bonaparte replied.

Monsieur de Talleyrand chuckled. 'You nearly killed Urquijo once, sire.'

Bonaparte looked at him incredulously.

'Did I never tell you what Urquijo did when, as chargé d'affaires in London, he first heard that by the Peace of Tolentino, and thanks to the intervention of the Spanish ambassador Azara, you had spared the papal government? Urquijo's reaction was really very odd. He ran out of his house like a maniac and for more than a mile along the Uxbridge road and then, in despair, he threw himself into a pond.'

'I find that story very difficult to believe.'

'So did I at the time, but my informant heard it from the lips of the surgeon who attended to Señor Urquijo, a Mr Carlisle, who happened to be passing when Urquijo was dragged out from the pond unconscious and who supervised his recovery by means recommended by the English Humane Society.'

'Nevertheless,' objected Bonaparte, 'Urquijo was intent on much needed reforms in Spain, such as the suppression of the Inquisition and several monastic institutions.'

'Maybe, but he went about them too clumsily and he removed from office too many experienced men who might have been persuaded to support him eventually. They say, but I am merely reporting rumours, that Urquijo, who is a handsome man, slighted the Queen's advances and ostentatiously preferred the Princess Branciaforte, sister of the Prince of the Peace, his most dangerous rival. Anyway, this much is certain: Urquijo's plan to appoint a patriarch in Spain and withdraw submission to the Dataria in Rome seriously alarmed Charles IV, who feared the prospect of a schism in the church. The Nuncio himself presented a remonstrance. No, I am afraid that Urquijo did not play his cards at all well. Incarceration is, I agree, an excessive measure to take against him but he had undoubtedly contributed to his downfall.'

'The Prince of the Peace will have to mend his dissembling ways if he wishes to prevent his own and even more ignominious downfall,' Bonaparte replied coldly. 'I wish that my reaction to his request for my portrait be conveyed to him without any ambiguity.'

Bonaparte believed that his remarks would serve to mitigate the sentence against Urquijo which was still being discussed in Madrid. It did nothing to help Urquijo, however, and Godoy was deeply offended by the personal insult.

After his stormy interview with Bonaparte, Monsieur de Talleyrand wrote to Lucien instructing him to reopen talks with the Portuguese so as to obtain better terms. France, he said, and that meant Bonaparte, refused to ratify the Treaty of Badajoz. Lucien replied that he could not possibly go back on his tracks, it would make his position untenable; he asked to be recalled – which was just what his brother wanted.

As for Godoy, when he learned that France refused to ratify the treaty, he suddenly turned insolent and insinuated that he could, if he wanted, make a separate peace with England.

Bonaparte called Azara, the Spanish ambassador in Paris, and asked him coldly: 'Are your sovereigns so tired of reigning, Señor Azara? If Godoy drags the King and Queen into measures contrary to the honour and interests of the French Republic, the last hour of the Spanish monarchy will have sounded.'

Talks began between France and Portugal which prompted Godoy to send a bellicose letter to Bonaparte on 26 July 1801:

His Spanish Majesty will consider the entry of French troops above the number of 15,000 fixed by treaty as a violation of his territory. The objective of the war against Portugal having been achieved, he desires the French troops to return to their country as rapidly as possible. [He demanded the return from Brest of the Spanish squadron and stated that Spain had suffered innumerable calamities caused by the war with Russia and England.]

Bonaparte, through Azara, threatened Spain with war and drew up a list of grievances against Godoy which made the favourite calm down and finally agree to a reconciliation. Monsieur de Talleyrand then drew up the clauses of the Treaty of Madrid, signed on 27 August 1801, whereby peace was declared with Portugal in exchange for an indemnity of twenty million reales and a number of Portuguese vessels which were to take part in the planned operation against Egypt.

Two months later, however, France gave up Egypt and Malta to England prior to the Peace of Amiens between the two countries; in return, England ceded her colonial conquests with the exception of Ceylon and she was allowed to retain Spanish Trinidad. Godoy sent an emissary to Paris to protest and ask for the restitution of Trinidad, but no notice was taken of his demand. The war against England, as France's ally, had cost Spain eleven ships and ruined her finances. She only hoped that the peace would last so as to enable her to restore her economy and resume her commerce with the Near East and her South American possessions. Goods and piastres began to flow once more from the colonies to Cadiz, unhampered by the English.

Charles IV had the characteristic Bourbon nose and chin. He was
virtuous, easy-going and benevolent, but preferred hunting to affairs
of state.

The Spanish royal family: in the foreground on the left, Ferdinand and his fiancée, Maria Antoineta of Naples; behind them, Carlos, Goya (in the shadows) and the king's sister, Maria Josefa; then, Maria Isabel, Queen Maria Luisa holding Francisco Paula by the hand and

Charles IV; behind, the king's brother, Antonio Pascual, and eldest daughter, Carlota; on the right, Luis of Parma (later Etruria) and his wife, Maria Luisa (Luisetta), holding her baby.

Queen Maria Luisa dressed as a *maja*, with her round white arm well
to the fore — her only attractive feature.

The new King and Queen of Etruria, Maria Luisa and Louis, had passed through Paris in 1801 on their way to their ephemeral kingdom; they had been fêted by Bonaparte, who had taken a malicious pleasure in exhibiting the pathetic couple to the French public. Thirteen-year-old Maria Luisa was ugly and had a deformed hip, Louis was mentally feeble and had an attack of epilepsy while on a visit to La Malmaison.

'Rome can be at ease – this one will not pass the Rubicon,' Bonaparte smiled.

Maria Luisa (Luisetta, as she was called in the family circle) had written to Godoy from Olmedo on 24 April:

My esteemed friend Manuel, forgive me for not writing to you before, but, as you may guess, I was in a sorry state at leaving my parents whom I have always loved, as you well know. I was also grieved to have to leave you, whom I have known since I was an infant, and who have always been so kind to me. I ask you to believe me when I say that I love you very much and ask you not to forget your true friend, Maria Luisa.

The Infanta wrote to Godoy again from Florence on 12 February 1802 with the unselfconscious frankness characteristic of so many ladies of the time:

I cannot conceal that I have a faint suspicion I may be pregnant. The first day I missed my period there was a ball, but I did not dance and I take great care of myself. I wish we had such a faithful friend as my beloved parents have in you.

Unlike her brother Ferdinand, Luisetta looked upon Godoy as a member of her family.

In October 1801, Lucien bid a touching farewell to The Kings, from whom he received presents of diamonds to the value of five million francs. His place was taken by General Gouvion de St Cyr.

Charles had not been well. He had had an attack of an unspecified nature and the new French ambassador was instructed to state that in the event of His Majesty's death France would only recognize Ferdinand as his heir. Rumours

had evidently reached Paris that Godoy was angling for a
Regency. Bonaparte was beginning to distrust him. The
double-deal after the War of the Oranges and their subsequent acrimonious exchange of correspondence had left
their mark. Napoleon was a Corsican; he did not easily forget
or forgive.

PART THREE

A DOUBLE WEDDING.
PRINCE FERDINAND INTRIGUES

X

In accordance with the terms of the treaty between France and England, signed in London on 1 October 1801 and ratified in Amiens in the following March, England was to evacuate Malta within three months and France was to occupy Taranto in the kingdom of Naples and maintain a garrison there. General Murat, Napoleon's brother-in-law, arrived there with the rank of ambassador extraordinary and dazzled everyone with his elegance and Byronic looks.

Monsieur Alquier was transferred from Florence to Naples where he had ample scope for his love of gossip. The Queen of Naples, Marie Caroline, daughter of the formidable Queen Maria Theresa of Austria, was a vivid character who led an active political and amorous life. Her husband Ferdinand was entirely under her thumb. Marie Caroline was so violently anti-French that, as Bonaparte once declared, the effects of her tongue and pen were equivalent to an entire enemy battalion. It is therefore difficult to give credence to the English ambassador, Drummond, when he said that the double Spanish-Neapolitan marriages were first suggested by Alquier.

Drummond was convinced – on this point he was right – that Bonaparte was anxious to drive the Hapsburgs from Italy and to substitute the Bourbons whom he had less cause to fear. This argument made sense, for the Bourbons were a pretty feeble lot: in Madrid reigned easy-going Charles, who was dominated by Godoy and inclined to be eccentric; Louis of Etruria was an epileptic, Carlota of Portugal a nonentity. When Josephine expressed her surprise to Bonaparte that the chief of a Republic should create a sovereign by making the Prince of Parma King of Etruria he told her: 'You don't see what my plans are. Discord will scatter hatred and division among the royal family. Believe me, I shall maintain the new kingdom I have carved only so long as it favours my designs.'

Drummond reported that the Queen of Spain had written to her sister-in-law the Queen of Naples (both ladies, incidentally, detested each other heartily but they had to think of their common dynasty) suggesting that all the branches of the House of Bourbon should unite, with the assistance of Austria and England, and endeavour to restrain the ambitions of France. Godoy too wrote in the same vein.

Marie Caroline was a fervent anglophile. Her Foreign Minister was an expatriate Englishman, General John Acton, who had served in the French navy and then under his uncle, Commander Acton, commander of the fleet of the Grand Duke of Tuscany. Sir William Hamilton (whose notorious Emma was on friendly terms with Marie Caroline) thought that Acton was still an Englishman at heart and he passed useful information to him.

One trait which Marie Caroline shared with Maria Luisa (and the latter's daughter Luisetta) was the frankness with which she wrote to her gentlemen friends. To the Neapolitan ambassador in Paris, Gallo, Marie Caroline described her operation for haemorrhoids in intimate detail, accompanied by what she herself described as 'two very indecent drawings – only your interest in my health can excuse my sending them to you'.

Whoever thought of the dual Bourbon alliance first, the idea must have been mooted some time during 1801 for that was when Goya painted his famous command picture of the Spanish royal family in which a young woman stands next to Ferdinand with her face averted. Goya had not seen the Prince's prospective bride and therefore could not paint her portrait.

What a tableau for posterity! The royal family must have been blind to accept and actually be pleased with such a cruelly penetrating character study. Charles occupies the centre of the picture, with one foot pointing forward, his head thrown back and a pompous expression on his vacant but benevolent face. He was then fifty-three and showing signs of obesity in spite of his active outdoor life. Beside him stands fifty-year-old Maria Luisa, bejewelled and décollettée, with her favourite diamond arrow stuck in her dark hair, a false smile on her hard, authoritarian face and her well-shaped arms well to the fore. Dumpy Ferdinand, with his short legs and gawky stance, resembles his mother facially but lacks – so far – her insolent expression; he looks stultified and immature. Luis, the King of Etruria, with his big mouth and round eyes, looks stupid; the Infanta Maria Josefa, the King's sister, resembles one of Goya's witches, and the big frightened face of Don Antonio, the King's brother, stares in the background like one of the hares he was in the habit of shooting at Aranjuez. The other Infantes stand a little in front of the royal couple: the Infanta Maria Isabella and the Infante Francisco de Paula, who bore what Lady Holland described two years later as 'an indecent likeness to the Prince of the Peace'. The artist hovers in the penumbra – superstitious Maria Luisa must have objected to the unlucky number of thirteen in the royal tableau – and he stands, brush in hand with a half-malicious, half-apologetic smile on his manly face; the Aragonese of earthy stock has all the character and strength that his puppet masters lack.

The averted head of Ferdinand's bride-to-be, Maria Antoineta of Naples, accurately expressed what that intelligent young woman thought of her husband when she met him for the first time in October 1802. This marriage and that of Maria Antoineta's brother, Francis, to the Infanta Maria Isabella, were celebrated by proxy. Francis, heir to the throne of Naples, had lost his first wife and could not bear his enforced chastity. Only ten days after her death he had written to General Acton saying that 'his long celibacy oppressed him.' Marie Caroline confessed to Gallo: 'I blush that this is my son.'

At first it was believed that the Kings of Naples would go to Spain to attend the double wedding in Barcelona, but second thoughts prevailed. The policies of the two branches of the Bourbons differed and they distrusted each other intensely. In the words of the omniscient Monsieur Alquier:

'The letters from Aranjuez merely announced great preparations for hunting and fishing and from all appearances this solemn reunion would have been more formidable to the wild animals of Spain than to politics. But, however insignificant, it would not suit Chevalier Acton. It was inevitable that old quarrels would be explained and that consequently both monarchs would be enlightened about many facts they had only dimly guessed before in which both the Queen and Chevalier Acton were so deeply involved that all three are anxious to keep them dark. The Minister has therefore clearly demonstrated to the King that the welfare of the state would suffer from his absence. Ferdinand, who is the one person in his kingdom least acquainted with affairs, has yielded to the force of this argument, but to soothe his brother's [Charles] impatience and regret, he has promised to go to Madrid for his daughter's first lying-in.' This event, however, was destined never to take place.

Maria Antoineta set out with her brother Francis and her sister-in-law Maria Luisa, who gave birth to a daughter on the stormy seas. Marie Caroline bade her daughter a tearful farewell and was full of forebodings:

I thought the grief would kill me [she wrote to Gallo] embracing her for the last time in my life. Breakfast, dinner, supper – all made my tears flow. I missed this dear child everywhere and was all the more worried because the weather at sea was bad.

The Spanish party had left Madrid in September, passed through Valencia and stopped at several coastal resorts on their way to Barcelona. Canon Escoiquiz, with whom the Prince continued to correspond, thought that this was a good opportunity for him to learn something about his own country; until then he had travelled very little. Before the journey, and in order to stir his apathetic pupil's interest, the Canon bought books on the geology and botany of Catalonia. These were delivered through Ferdinand's barber, Don Antonio Moreno, an educated man with a good knowledge of French. But as soon as the books were discovered by the Prince of the Peace's spies they were removed on the pretext that the King disapproved of them. Perhaps he thought that a bridal journey was not an occasion for a course in local geography.

In Barcelona Ferdinand was gratified by the warmth of the public's acclamations. People seemed to like him, to know that he was forcibly kept in the background. There was a noticeable coolness towards Godoy, who was quick to sense the antagonism of the masses.

Maria Isabella burst in to tears long before she set eyes on her bridegroom; she had no desire to leave Spain and her mother's skirts. 'Pull yourself together; an Infanta never cries in public,' Maria Luisa admonished her daughter severely.

Godoy surreptitiously handed her a lace-edged handkerchief. The gesture did not pass unnoticed by the crowds. It had been rumoured for a long time that the Infanta was his daughter.

At last the ship from Naples, bringing Maria Antoineta and her brother Francis, sailed slowly into the port of Barcelona to the accompaniment of salvoes and a gigantic firework display arranged by Don Sebastian Carrion of Valencia.

Ferdinand's bride, Maria Antoineta, was a pale, sickly-looking girl who already showed signs of the consumption that was to cause her premature death; but she was quick-witted, vivacious and full of charm. The impression produced by Ferdinand upon his bride was conveyed in a letter to her mother sent shortly after her arrival in Spain: 'He is as stolid as a young bull, utterly dull and stupid.' When she first set eyes on him she thought she would faint.

Her mother wept when she read this description. 'I did not think he was quite as bad as that,' she replied. 'In the little portrait that was sent to us the Prince looked almost handsome. His eyes, in particular, were bright and black. The artist must have wished to soften the blow. Alas, my poor, dear daughter, how I feel for you!'

In one intimate respect, however, the Princess was not importuned by her boy husband. The wedding was not consummated in the large bridal bed made by the cabinet-maker Harzenbusch and conveyed to Barcelona for the newly-wedded couple.

Marie Caroline informed Gallo sadly:

The Prince of Asturias has an ugly face, a tubby figure, round knees and legs, a piping, delicate voice, and is quite unintelligent. Though he is physically amorous, they are not yet husband and wife, after sleeping together for a week. He is disagreeable, dull, as lazy as his sister, and he never leaves his wife for a single moment. He has no education, an unpleasant continuous giggle and their existence is cramped, without comforts or amenities, and subjected to scandalous espionage. Poor Antoinette sends me letters that make me weep. She writes: 'Mother, you have been deceived. For you are too good a mother to have sacrificed me like this if you had known. I shall not live, but I wish to behave well and deserve eternal life.' The day her brother left she implored him hysterically: 'I beseech you, take me away or kill me.' I think it monstrous that San Teodoro [the Neapolitan ambassador in Madrid] should have dared to deceive us so. He has been extremely impertinent to my daughter. I must thank God that I did not go to Barcelona, for I should have brought my children back without concluding the marriages, unable to sacrifice them, and all Europe would have cast stones at me.

Maria Antoineta produced an unfavourable impression upon her mother-in-law, who despised her for her weakly physique and was alarmed by her wit and powers of observation. The young Princess appeared to have a mind of her own and she refused to comply with Spanish court protocol. Maria Luisa soon began to voice her complaints. As she had guessed, Maria Antoineta had been well primed by her mother before she left Naples.

You must report to me in invisible ink [Marie Caroline ordered her] all that goes on at court and in particular the references you hear to relations with France . . . in brief, anything that may be useful to my allies the English, who will support your husband Ferdinand when the time comes. Has he got many supporters in Madrid? If so, tell me who they are and whether they are influential.

Maria Antoineta replied:

No, there is no such thing yet as a Prince's party. He has a few staunch friends among the grandees who detest the Prince of the Peace almost as much as he does, but for different reasons. *They* cannot bear him for being a vulgar upstart and for his lack of aristocratic background. Ferdinand, in addition to these, has other more personal reasons for his active dislike – nay, hatred – of the favourite. The people, too, are on our side. We are cheered whenever we show ourselves in public, which is not often, for the Queen is jealous. I try to be civil to her but she repulses me. She sees that I am beginning to exercise a beneficial influence on her son and that she cannot tolerate for she has done her utmost, and persuaded the King to follow suit, to rob Ferdinand of all initiative and personality. She is very much like a vampire. Godoy encourages her. Ferdinand is the chief obstacle to the climax of his career. I do believe he aims at nothing less than a crown; he is already the master of Spain but he is over-reaching himself. He is hated. That is our main hope for the future.

You *must* form a party [Marie Caroline advised her daughter]. You will need more than a handful of 'staunch friends' and vague public support when Charles dies and Ferdinand ascends the throne. I know it is not easy since you are watched by the Queen and her paramour, but begin to assemble those friends you have. Social gatherings in your apartments can cover useful discussions. Ideas can be formulated with respect to the composition of the future Council of State. Godoy must have placed his stooges in all the key positions and they will have to be replaced when the time comes. You must be well prepared for this eventuality.

'It is certain,' the French ambassador Beurnonville informed Monsieur de Talleyrand in March 1803, 'that the young Princess's steps are guided by her mother.'

Marie Caroline observed to her daughter in a more intimate vein:

I cannot help wondering what kind of a king that husband of yours will make. He sounds so heavy and uninspiring. How can a young man be so utterly lacking in interests and curiosity? You tell me that he spends hours in your room doing absolutely nothing. What a bore! My poor, poor child! Are you sure he is quite *normal*?

Maria Antoineta was in fact beginning to have doubts. While she had been thankful not to have to submit to Ferdinand's embraces on their wedding night, and he still did not attract her physically, she did want, and was expected to produce, children. Did Ferdinand know how? Incredible though it seemed, the young Prince had not manifested the slightest erotic desire, had never trespassed upon her half of the bed, and he appeared to be perfectly content to talk to his wife one half of the night and to snore soundly during the other. Such a state of affairs could not continue, but Maria Antoineta did not know how to broach the subject with her husband.

Finally she sought advice from her mother who reacted anxiously:

Is what you tell me about your husband *possible*? I find it hard to credit and I am filled with foreboding. Can it be that that great booby is impotent? Heaven forbid! That would be the last straw. I do not know what to suggest. Of course it would be most indelicate for *you* to make the first move. You have done all you *decently* could. Words fail me. What a predicament! Six months married and still no consummation . . . I am very worried. I shall write to San Teodoro. You tell me that Ferdinand likes him and that he is now one of your little group. This should make things easier. I shall ask him to have a heart to heart talk with your husband and to tell him where his duty lies. People must be beginning to wonder. They may blame *you*.

In fact, the Prince's 'piping, delicate voice' and unresponsiveness were due to his physical immaturity. He was shaved for the first time on 15 May 1803.

At last, in the middle of September, the Duke of San Teodoro was able to announce to Marie Caroline that the marriage had been consummated. Maria Antoineta was soon enceinte. The news spread like wildfire round the palace of the Escorial where the court assembled at the end of the year.

Maria Antoineta shivered with apprehension at the prospect of another sojourn in that bleakest of all the royal residences although it was pierced by no less than twelve hundred windows, for there the living walked above the dead laid out in the pantheon beneath the church in the centre of the great granite building in the form of a gridiron, to commemorate the martyrdom of St Lawrence.

Built by Philip II with bluish-grey stones from the surrounding sierra of the Guadarrama, the royal apartments had been a secondary consideration in the mind of their founder, who had attached far more importance to the monastery of Hieronymite monks, the church and the cloister comprised within the vast enclosure. The spirit of the morose monarch, who had died here slowly and in great pain, haunted the draughty corridors, the sixteen courtyards, the eighty-six stairways.

Charles spent most of his time in the gracious Casita del Principe, a pavilion decorated in Louis XVI style, built for him by his father Charles III in the gardens below the palace. Don Antonio, his brother, escaped to the pavilion known as the Casita de Arriba, on the road to the six thousand feet high Pic d'Albartes that towered above San Lorenzo, as the palace of the Escorial was generally referred to. The extensive views of rocky mountains, isolated boulders scattered between hummocks of aromatic plants in the spring, and barren tableland, was satisfying only to seekers of the absolute. Chateaubriand called it the 'Versailles of the steppes'.

XI

The Queen had taken to the uncomfortable habit — for the newly-married pair — of slipping unannounced into their private apartments and of looking round suspiciously as if she hoped to discover some sinister plot. This was particularly disconcerting to Maria Antoineta in her delicate condition. A few days after the court had settled at San Lorenzo Maria Antoineta described in a letter to her mother the disagreeable scene which had taken place between her and her mother-in-law.

Maria Luisa had walked into her room and asked for Ferdinand. The Prince was in bed with a cold, so the Queen took Maria Antoineta aside and engaged in a tête-à-tête. She was shocked, she told her, to have overhead her say the night

before at supper that she had not yet visited the royal
Pantheon of San Lorenzo built by Philip II for his remains
and those of his successors.

Maria Antoineta was far from anxious to look at tombs;
the Escorial as a whole was dreary enough and even colder
than the other royal palaces, but the Queen insisted. The
Pantheon, she stressed, was a splendid and original underground building; she herself had first set eyes on it soon after
her arrival in Spain from Italy — she was only fourteen at the
time — and it had been shown to her by her father-in-law,
Charles III, who impressed upon her that she must consider it
as part of Spain's royal heritage and be proud of the privilege
of being buried there when the time came.

The Queen led the reluctant Princess into the sombre
church at the foot of the stairs, opened a door off the passage
leading to the sacristy, and groped her way to a shelf upon
which were a couple of oil lamps which she proceeded to
light.

She then led the way down thirty-four steps to the first
landing and the entrance to the vault called the *pudridero,*
the rotting-place, where the bodies of Kings and Queens had
to lie for ten years before being transferred to the Pantheon
proper.

At the bottom of a further flight of marble stairs, the
Queen tiptoed round the octagonal-shaped room, about
thirty-two feet in diameter and a little more in height,
decorated with jasper, porphyry and rose marble, set off by a
profusion of gilt bronze ornaments. On each side of the altar
set into the centre wall were two rows of superimposed black
marble niches with a scroll on the front of each bearing the
name of the sovereign whose remains were inside. She
pointed out how small these niches were and explained that
that was the reason for the *pudridero* upstairs. The bones had
to be broken up into pieces and packed closely in order to
fit. The corpses had therefore to be well and truly rotted and
the bones brittle. The Kings were placed on the right, the
Queens on the left-hand side.

Maria Luisa took the Princess to the Pantheon of the Infantes which was simple compared to that of the Kings, but moving in that it contained the tombs of children and Infantas who had died in childbirth without leaving any succession.

Maria Antoineta was shown the row of tombs set against the low walls, the red marble plaques inscribed with the names of their occupants and the armorial bearings beneath them.

'You will occupy the space next to mine in the Pantheon,' Maria Luisa informed her. Maria Antoineta followed her to the far end of the Pantheon where, on the floor before a rotunda containing more tombs of Infantas, lay a highly-polished mahogany coffin. The Queen observed that it should be a perfect fit because her measurements had been sent to the royal coffin-maker the day that Maria Antoineta arrived in Spain. The little Princess was horrified.

'They were thinking of my demise from the moment I landed,' she wrote to her mother.

The Queen had added: 'Wherever we may be when death finally overtakes us, our miserable remains will be collected and brought here to rest until eternity among the other members of our dynasty. You are still only an Infanta and so your coffin must stay here for the time being with the other Infantas. My coffin is in another vault but no doubt one day we shall lie beside each other at peace in the Pantheon of Kings.'

This, however, was not to be.

Lady Holland visited San Lorenzo in the company of her husband not long after this scene had taken place. She found it 'solid, dull and gloomy beyond imagination', as she wrote in her diary.

An aspect heightened by the fact that the heavens were darkened by clouds, a heavy storm was approaching. The only walks are the cloisters and the Princess of Asturias skips about the sacristy and the church to amuse herself.

She caught another glimpse of the Princess in the gardens of La Granja:

She is very little, rather pretty, with a strong resemblance to her mother, the Queen of Naples. The Duchess of San Teodoro, her lady-in-waiting, accompanies the Princess in her walks through the leafy promenades. The royal family drive up and down the centre of the walks preceded by a detachment of gardes de corps, followed by the Infantes, lords and ladies, pages, the court physician and surgeon. Godoy followed with his Princess.

She found Godoy

large, coarse, ruddy-complexioned, with a heavy, sleepy, voluptuous eye. He passes a week alternately at the Madrid palace and here, one for the voice and support of the Queen, the other to secure the silence and obedience of his first and legal wife, the Tudó, whom he both loves and fears. The situation is an enigma — no one has the key to the riddle.

Lord Holland attended one of Godoy's levees in Madrid and found the anti-chamber crowded with

all that is great and distinguished and beautiful, and, tho' often fatigued by their servility, his [Godoy's] manner never offends. It is impossible with truth to ascertain what are the ties between him and the Queen. He has the King' s confidence independently of her influence and yet whenever he is hard pressed by unpopularity or by French interference she supports him effectually — for instance recently in the case of a letter written by Bonaparte in which his dismissal was made a specific condition. The people of Madrid call Godoy 'El Bonducani', the nickname of the Caliph at which all bow, obey and tremble.

Bonaparte accused him of placing large funds in the hands of their common enemy the English . . . this charge Godoy mentioned publicly at his levee, saying that it was preposterous and ill-founded. This in truth he could not well do, as from a circumstance it has come to my knowledge that he has sums to a considerable amount in our stocks.

Lady Holland was presented to the Queen by the Duchess of San Teodoro, wife of the Neapolitan ambassador. She appeared at court without gloves

as that species of clothing produces such a sudden and violent physical effect upon the King that the Queen alone chooses to encounter the consequences. White leather gloves produce similar effects upon many of the Spanish branches of the Bourbon family.

The Queen's manner is uncommonly gracious; she shows great readiness in making conversation, and taste in choosing her topics. All she said was flattering, obliging and well-expressed. The King is a good-natured person whose talents lie in the skill of the chase.

During the presentation the Queen

called her favourite child, the Infante Don Francisco, born in 1794, a pretty, lively boy bearing a most indecent likeness to Godoy. She enumerated the children she had had and those she had lost and then she called for Ferdinand, adding: 'My eldest son, whom you are going to see, you will find ugly; he is the counterpart of myself.'

The Queen begged Lady Holland to go back in the evening to see her diamonds,

for which she has a royal fondness . . . From there we went to the Princess of Asturias and the Prince . . . a gawky lad like the Bentincks. The little Princess is very agreeable in her manner.

She was in mourning for Louis, the young King of Etruria, who had just died, leaving Luisetta a widow. Maria Luisa, her mother, was sure that he had been frightened to death by the French who hemmed them in from all sides.

Lady Holland commented with amusement on the archaic etiquette of the Spanish court:

The King and the little Infantes are served with drinks by gentlemen-in-waiting on their knees. The old custom is retained of tasting what the King and Queen are to drink and eat. When a cup is carried through the apartments or corridors of the palace, everyone by whom it passes must take off his hat. At the Escorial lately, one obstinate fellow refused to salute the bearer of the cup, whereupon the latter threw it down, exclaiming: 'The cup has been insulted', and the man responsible was imprisoned. A gentleman-in-waiting scratches the King's back at night in bed and the Lord Chamberlain puts on the King's shirt.

The Hollands spent several evenings in the houses of the anglophile aristocrats who were forming what came to be known as the 'Fernandino party'. It was a very limited circle. The leading light was the Duke of Infantado who had been educated in France and had many interests. These embraced agriculture – he took a personal interest in his vast northern estates and in the breeding of merinos (whose wool, he told the Hollands, loses its excellent quality after a generation or two) — machinery, minerals, fossils, chemical instruments, porcelain, books on armoury and Mexican manuscripts. The Duke clung to a mistress who was a commoner and Lady Holland observed that high society, such as it was, reproach-ed him for his lack of taste. 'One cannot but regret,' she noted in her journal, 'that an obscure connection deprives society of his example and talents.' The Duke was soon, however, to play an important role in the Prince's entourage and the chain of events that were to plunge Spain into war and disaster.

XII

When the hereditary Prince of Naples returned from Barce-lona with his child bride the Infanta Maria Isabella, every-body gasped. The King, according to Marie Caroline, was 'amazed by her . . . She is as little and as round as a ball. She has a fine, healthy face, fresh, not Bourbon in the least, but white and red, with black eyes. She is very stout and sturdy, yet her legs are very short. So much for her exterior. The rest cannot be described because I myself cannot understand it. She is null in every respect: knowledge, ideas, curiosity. Nothing, absolutely nothing. She speaks a little Spanish, but neither Italian nor French and only monosyllables: yes or no, indiscriminately. She smiles all the time, whether she is pleased or not. Francis's child aged four has far more intelligence. It is incredible. Ferdinand has engaged masters to teach her Italian and the rudiments of geography and arithmetic. She knows nothing except a little piano. I have tried to praise and enliven her. She feels nothing, she merely laughs. It is an automaton which might acquire certain attitudes, but never real maturity. I try every means to mould her as a companion for her husband, even if this may turn her against myself. Believe me, this child is a tough present, for she will neither ennoble nor improve our race. My son behaves very well and treats her kindly, but he is revolted, bored and disgusted to the last degree by the Court of Spain and all he has seen and heard there of crime, triumphant vice, magnificence in appearances but emptiness in reality. It is to this infamous brothel that I have had the misfortune to sacrifice my daughter, my darling Maria Antoineta.'

As time went on, however, both parties became more used to one another. The Duchesse d'Abrantes described in her memoirs of the court of Spain that Ferdinand and his bride were very close and that

the attachment of these unfortunate young people was the only alleviation they found in a life of constant trouble and vexations. Always when they are together the Prince follows with his eyes those of the Princess that he may be guided in what he is to do. She is not pretty . . . some even consider her plain; it is possible, but to me she appears pretty and graceful.

One of the many 'troubles and vexations' referred to by the Duchess was Maria Luisa's constant interference and malevolent espionage. She developed the aggravating habit of walking into her son's private apartments quietly and unannounced. Did she hope thereby to overhear the whispered intrigues, the schemes devised by what came to be known as 'the Neapolitan party' led by Maria Antoineta and remotely controlled by the Queen of Naples?

Marie Caroline wrote to Gallo complaining of the

infamous conduct of the Spanish court with Maria Antoineta . . . after the condescendence we have had with the little epileptic bastard whom we possess and whom I love [she had changed her attitude towards her little daughter-in-law since she had come to know her better] because she is good, and it isn't her fault if she was conceived in crime and wickedness.

Maria Antoineta had effected a noticeable change in her husband. He had become surer of himself, more sociable and alert. It was rumoured that the young couple occasionally invited the English ambassador to their private parties.

Lady Holland made several references in her journal to this ineffectual ambassador transferred from Lisbon to Madrid, John Hookham Frere — a friend of Pitt, former editor of the *Anti Jacobin*, a poetaster who frequented literary rather than political circles and whose Anglo-Saxon reserve did not help to improve relations between Spain and England.

The Treaty of Amiens between England and France had only been, to use George III's expression, 'an experimental peace'. Hostilities were resumed in May 1803. Bonaparte needed money to prosecute the war and pursue his bellicose plans on several fronts. At the beginning of May he sold Louisiana to the United States for eighty million francs, a transaction which greatly irritated Charles. He exclaimed to Godoy: 'We must beware of those rascally French who have sold Louisiana to the Americans for a mere bagatelle after they had promised that they would never do so. We have the right, in these circumstances, to remain neutral.'

Foreign Minister Lord Hawkesbury instructed Frere 'to endeavour to separate Spain from France. This is to be the constant and persevering object of all your attention.' If it proved impossible Frere was to try to secure Spain's neutrality. This coincided with the Spanish Kings' wishes, but Frere played his cards badly. His first interview at court went off well but he was inclined to promise too much. Godoy reported to the Queen: 'The English offer is tremendous. I have mentioned Trinidad and Gibraltar, as the price of our eventual neutrality . . . we are fawned upon, Madam . . . '

Godoy believed himself to be in a favourable position but Bonaparte's threats soon dispelled his illusions. A Spanish financier established in Paris, José Martinez Hervas, was used as a go-between in a secret convention negotiated between The Kings, Bonaparte and Monsieur de Talleyrand, who — as usual — profited from his participation in the talks. Monsieur de Talleyrand, like his master, needed money, but for very different purposes. Bonaparte lived like a general. His Foreign Minister lived like a little king in an ambience of gold and silver plate, rustling silks, delicate perfumes and witty women. He had 'class' and Bonaparte was aware that his dazzling aura of prestige could be useful. 'You must buy yourself a splendid domain, Monsieur de Talleyrand,' he told him, 'where you can suitably receive foreign diplomats'; in 1803 he helped Talleyrand to buy the beautiful palace of Valençay surrounded by parks and woods. Its upkeep cost a small fortune, so de Talleyrand seized the chance presented to him by the negotiations that preceded France's Subsidies Treaty with Spain.

Five million francs a month. That was the sum demanded by France in exchange for Spain's neutrality, despite her protests that it was far too much and that she could not afford it. Godoy had hesitated before signing the treaty. 'Is it a service to render one's King and country to submit to such a heavy burden?' he confided to Frere.

Señor Azara, who was on good terms with Lord Whitworth, the British ambassador in Paris, kept the latter informed of what was going on, but not of the exact amount of the subsidy. The English government was assured that Spain was acting under compulsion, not from illwill towards England. Later in the year, however, when the details leaked out, Frere declared that the magnitude of the sum amounted to a war subsidy and was a mark of hostility against Great Britain. The treaty was prejudicial to British interests, he said openly, and dangerous to British dominions.

At first Godoy tried to placate England. 'Prudence prompts us to see what the British reaction to the subsidies will be,' he wrote to the Queen, and in London the Spanish ambassador Anduaga held long talks with Hawkesbury and the Prime Minister, Viscount Addington, to discuss how far Spain could help France without violating her neutrality. At the end of December, Frere told Godoy that a temporary subsidy would be countenanced, but not a permanent one.

Spain was so slow in paying up that she provoked Bonaparte into one of his rages. He told Hervas brutally: 'Your government puts so much illwill in all it does for

France that it forces me to take violent measures which make me lose time ... I can quite understand that the Spanish people entertain that natural animosity against us which is common to neighbouring countries, but such passions are unworthy of Ministers. There is nothing new in the Spanish attitude. The files of Versailles are full of correspondence in the same vein. If Spain had been more flexible, the unfortunate Louis XVI would still be alive ... you would render a great service to your country if you could convince the Ministry of this truth.'

In August 1803 Bonaparte even threatened to cross the Pyrenees if no subsidy was forthcoming, but in fact he had no serious intentions at that moment of invading Spain. On 23 September he wrote to General Beurnonville in Madrid: 'Maybe the resistance of which the Spaniards are capable would carry us beyond the goal for which we had originally penetrated into their territory.' Still the possibility of entering Spain had, momentarily at least, crossed his mind.

Rumours had reached him about the dissensions within the Spanish royal family. The Spanish ambassador in Paris, Señor Azara, had written a sarcastic letter to Don Pedro Cevallos, the Secretary of State, about Godoy, and this reached the favourite's ears. Azara was recalled in November 1803. Bonaparte now realized the full extent of Godoy's importance in Spanish affairs.

Yet Godoy was beginning to feel insecure. Charles had had another bout of the mysterious malady that had afflicted him the year before and for which he had been bled twice. It was described as an attack of fever accompanied by rheumatic pains, but since the King appeared to have become more vague and apathetic than usual after the illness one suspects that it must have been more in the nature of a stroke. Another source reported that he had suffered an apoplectic fit.

The Hollands, who were still in Madrid at the beginning of 1804, heard about the current intrigues through their various anglophile friends and Caballero, Minister of Grace and

Justice, who was approached to participate in a plot to disinherit the Prince of Asturias. It was believed that the Council of Castile, no doubt through the instigation of the Queen and Godoy, had been consulted as to how this could be accomplished with propriety and that the council had replied: 'there was no known authority which could deprive a Prince of Asturias, duly sworn, married and honoured, of his right of succession.'

Lady Holland observed in her journal:

Indiscreet language was used in the apartment of the Prince of Asturias during the King's illness at the Escorial, which naturally enough had indisposed the old court towards the young one. Great apprehensions are entertained about the future reign; shoals of Italians, especially of Neapolitans, have arrived, hoping to bask in the sunshine of their native protectress. The Neapolitan embassy are viewed with dislike and pique by both courts. The Princess is supposed already to have collected among her countrymen a favourite, Louis Caffara, a garde du corps.

As soon as the King was better, Lady Holland went on, an architect was sent to Badajoz near the Portuguese frontier to prepare a residence for the court in the following October. 'The Queen's project means a palace for a retreat at some future period. Godoy has frankly declared his intention of returning to his native Estremadura after the death of the King.' Crown lands were bestowed upon him and the right to have his heirs bear the title of Prince.

They call it here a *billet d'enterrement du roi* [advance note on the King's burial] as it confirms the belief in his illness and of approaching danger. It is a proof of the vanity and egotism of Godoy to imagine that such a measure would bind hereafter Ferdinand should he be inclined to pluck this fat bird . . . Fresh taxes and scarcity press upon every class. Godoy is unaccountable in his conduct towards Ferdinand; instead of conciliating him by tokens of respect, he offends and has insulted him by slights and has made of him an implacable enemy who will not delay showing his resentment by overturning this rival whose only ambition is to amass immense wealth and whose habitual and constant indolence impede the execution of any great enterprise. Not only is he without a party or adherents but he has no friend upon whom he can rely.

Godoy sensed this isolation himself and began to be alarmed. The people blamed him for all the calamities that had afflicted them during the past months, even for the earthquake that had shaken Valencia and whose tremors were felt as far inland as Madrid. One day he heard a sound of crashing glass on the landing outside his study. He ran out and found his servants hastily picking up the fragments from the broken window overlooking the street. One of the servants picked up another object which had been hurled through the window.

'What is it?' Godoy asked. The servant silently held out his hand. In it was a loaf of bread cut into four quarters. A small knife held a note pinned to the middle which read: 'Godoy! One day this will happen to you.'

'Have all the windows boarded up immediately,' he ordered. For three days after this incident he stayed indoors, not daring to show his face to the public.

To whom could he turn for support? It was rumoured that Bonaparte intended to march his troops through Spain to reach Portugal. John Frere rashly promised English aid but, as Godoy exclaimed with a gesture of despair: 'What can England do for us?'

Frere had observed a great deal of activity in several Spanish ports and he had heard of a French plan to annex Portugal to Spain in exchange for the northern provinces of Spain above the River Ebro. Who was double-crossing whom?

On the strength of Frere's dispatches, the diplomatist Lord Malmesbury wrote in his diary:

Spain is on the eve of a revolution – not a French, but a Spanish revolution, so very unpopular are the court and government, that is to say the Queen and the Prince of the Peace. I asked Frere: 'Supposing we had 20,000 disposable men whether such a force would be equal to produce this Spanish revolution and to prevent Bonaparte from availing himself of it?' Frere did not doubt it. He said the people were more anti-French than ever and if they had Ministers in whom they could confide and the King was left to himself, he was persuaded, with the sort of force I mentioned, Spain might be saved and become a close, steady and most useful friend and ally to England.

As Bonaparte asked Spain for naval support and naval armaments proceeded apace in Spanish ports, Frere was instructed to make complaints 'but not to drive matters precipitately to extremity, to leave an opening for conciliation and arrangement'. These tactics were beyond Frere's limited diplomatic talents; he only succeeded in provoking Godoy and causing a scene. It was finally considered prudent to have him recalled.

Godoy was not displeased. Not only did he doubt very much whether the English could be counted upon – they were too far away, while the French were on Spain's doorstep – but he also suspected that they would be more inclined to favour Ferdinand, his anglophile wife and his even more anglophile mother-in-law Marie Caroline of Naples than him.

XIII

Bonaparte's star continued to rise and in June 1804 he hoisted it by having himself crowned Emperor at Notre Dame. Bonaparte became Napoleon I and as such the prospective founder of a dynasty. Josephine, who had passed the age of child-bearing, sensing that her future was doomed shed tears during the coronation service.

A detailed description of the impressive ceremony was sent to The Kings by the new ambassador in Paris, Admiral Gravina. Its implications were discussed with Godoy who made up his mind to play the French game, for a personal consideration. He had already, as Lady Holland observed, contemplated a passive 'retreat' in Estremadura, but better still, as a security for an uncertain future with Ferdinand on the throne, would be his own private kingdom carved out of Portugal in return for Spanish aid directed against that ill-starred pawn. Not another War of the Oranges. This time there would be no bluff. His scheme would have to be placed before the Emperor by a trusted envoy, a personal friend, not by the official ambassador. It was expedient at this preliminary juncture to keep the project secret, even from the King. One may assume, however, that the Queen had been taken into his confidence.

Godoy therefore invited his friend, the well-known Spanish botanist Señor Izquierdo, to visit him at Aranjuez. Godoy's genuine interest in botany and his experimental nursery at San Lucar de Barrameda have already been referred to. Together the two friends sauntered through the beautiful, still gardens that bordered the Tagus, where there was no possibility of being overheard. Izquierdo had connections in Paris, particularly with a distinguished French colleague, Monsieur Lacépède. This famous French botanist and scientist was Monsieur de Talleyrand's protégé. And Monsieur de Talleyrand was still the Emperor's all-powerful adviser. So Godoy appointed Izquierdo to act as his personal envoy and agent in Paris. In the meantime he would set about looking for a quarrel with Lisbon. The knowledge that the Princess of Asturias was pregnant may have been an additional spur to Godoy to assure his future.

Maria Luisa kept Godoy informed of the correspondence which she and her daughter-in-law received from Marie Caroline who frequently complained about the secluded life that Maria Antoineta was obliged to lead at the court of Spain. 'I enclose the letter I received last night from the Queen of Naples,' Maria Luisa wrote to Godoy on 29 November,

from which you can see that she again comes back to the subject of her daughter; she had been quiet for some time after I had told her that mine too was in a foreign country. I want you to advise me whether I should say more about this and that her daughter should adapt herself to our customs, forgetting those of other countries, as my daughter is doing in Italy, remarking, too, on the indecency of Maria Antoineta's dresses. Tell me what you think I should do. One needs a great deal of patience to bear with these vexations. I think it would be wise to send back Maria Antoineta's ladies-in-waiting who are a party to all the intrigues going on behind our backs. Our daughter is alone over there. We can either inform the ambassador or write to the Queen.

In November 1804 the Princess of Asturias had a miscarriage which Maria Luisa described to Godoy from the very first symptoms:

My daughter-in-law stayed in bed today with belly pains, which began last night. As every month she has pains but nothing more we don't know what they can be due to.

Two days later she added:

I have just been present at the miscarriage of my daughter-in-law. She had some pain and a little blood flowed, but not even as much as one day of my menstrual flow. The foetus was smaller than a grain of aniseed and the umbilical cord was as thin as a cobweb. The King had to put on his glasses to see it . . .

It had already been reported to The Kings that the Prince of Asturias and his wife had received the English ambassador several times before his recall. A little while after the Princess's miscarriage court spies observed another visitor who began to pay regular calls. These were vividly described later in his memoirs.

A tall, bearded man in a dark suit, carrying a bundle of newspapers under his arm, loped up the concealed staircase leading to the back of the Prince's apartments in the royal palace of Madrid. The sentries allowed him to pass; most of them knew that he was not the antiquarian bookseller he purported to be but Canon Escoiquiz in an unconvincing disguise. He could not alter his height and he made no attempt to change his characteristic gait. The Canon, who delighted in intrigue, was quite sure, however, that nobody recognized him.

He was shown into the Prince's private study overlooking the pine-studded Casa de Campo. While he waited, he took the newspapers from under his arm, spread them on a table under one of the windows and, drawing a pencil from his pocket, began to tick off several of the articles.

When Ferdinand entered the Canon noticed that his face was drawn and anxious.

'I trust Her Royal Highness is better?' he inquired.

Ferdinand shook his head. 'I am afraid not. She does not seem to be able to recover from her miscarriage although the mishap occurred weeks ago.'

'It was a great disappointment,' said the Canon. 'I hope that the sausage merchant has had nothing to do with it.'

'I do not think so. We are very careful about what we eat and drink. Every item is tasted beforehand by my valet Pedro.'

'He may have become immune to poison.'

'No, I am of the opinion that my mother is to blame. She gave Maria Antoineta a terrible shock when she took her down to the vaults of the Escorial to show her the coffin set aside for her. She was perfectly aware that my wife is very impressionable and that it was bound to have a profound affect upon her. She was right. Ever since that day my wife has woken up in the middle of the night, trembling and sobbing.'

'The English press attributes the miscarriage to the machinations of both the sausage merchant and your mother. I have brought you the articles.' The Canon proceeded to translate them.

'What a pity,' sighed the Prince, 'that Napoleon has forced us to declare war on England. [This had taken place in December 1804.] Even my father was not eager to do so. Still, after the incidents at Ferrol and Cadiz last autumn, he could hardly do otherwise. The blockade of the French force at Ferrol was carried out by Admiral Cochrane with scant respect for our rights as a neutral.'

'Yes, but,' objected the Canon, 'I have been informed on good authority that his conduct was prompted by the hostile attitude of our people. They had given assistance to French privateers and were seen to be fitting out a large number of ships in the dockyards. The sausage merchant is behind all that, of course.'

'But what about the piratical act of the English off Cadiz when they summoned our four treasure ships from the Americas to surrender and then captured three ships with booty valued at a million pounds? That was inexcusable!'

'True, but the English had warned us that any serious armaments on our part would lead to war without further negotiations or notice. I admit that they are never slow to seize a profitable opportunity; it is always the way when a nation commands superior forces and we are not in a position to retaliate.'

The conversation was interrupted by the appearance of Maria Antoineta. She held a letter in her hand. The Canon was shocked to see the change in her looks since his last visit. She was as thin as a wraith and her pale blue eyes shone with an unnatural brilliance. She walked as slowly as an old woman, yet she was barely twenty-three. He rose to greet her, then he showed her the articles in the English newspapers. Maria Antoineta was better educated than her husband and she could read English. She smiled with pleasure.

'My mother is certainly responsible for the information contained in those articles,' she said. 'When I was told that you had arrived, Canon, I wrote a letter to tell her about our latest deliberations. Would you please give it to the usual courier for transmission? I take it that he is reliable? You have no doubts on that score?'

The Canon took the letter, folded it carefully and placed it in a secret pocket in the lining of his jacket.

'The courier is absolutely reliable, Your Royal Highness. I would stake my life on it,' he replied emphatically.

The courier entrusted with Maria Antoineta's letter to her mother in Naples was indeed reliable but an accident occurred en route. Napoleon's chief of police, Fouché, disposed of a wide network of spies and informers all over Europe.

Napoleon was at St Cloud when an aide-de-camp brought him a copy of Maria Antoineta's intercepted letter. A convincing story had been put abroad to the effect that the Neapolitan courier from Madrid had been thrown from his horse a few miles from the French frontier by a bandit who made off with his wallet and dispatch case. The courier informed the local police and stayed in a cockroach-infested inn for two days, at the end of which, to his immense relief and astonishment, his effects were recovered. He continued his journey after having praised the police and rewarded them handsomely for their pains. They pocketed the money and omitted to tell the courier that a 'shepherd' had returned the stolen objects. The shepherd did not mind; he would receive ample compensation for having borrowed and copied the incriminating letter . . .

Napoleon had the letter sent to Izquierdo who in turn forwarded it to Godoy. It was a good opportunity to demand more naval assistance from the recalcitrant Spaniards. How slow they were, how inefficient! 'Spain will have to be dragged into the nineteenth century by the scruff of the neck,' Napoleon declared. But he realized that to achieve this objective he would have to humour Godoy by displaying an interest in his scheme for the partition of Portugal. In any case it happened to coincide with his own plans, more or less. As usual the Emperor's mind darted in several directions at once.

The Queen of Naples' reply to her daughter was intercepted by Godoy's agents. It was more violent and compromising than he had dared to hope and the favourite, in his turn, forwarded a copy to Napoleon.

As for Maria Luisa, she almost went into hysterics when she read what Marie Caroline had written about her and dear Manuel. 'Your mother-in-law and Godoy should be poisoned,' the Queen of Naples had suggested more wildly than realistically. Godoy's indignation matched that of the Queen. 'This hotbed of intrigue is threatening the stability of the crown and must be suppressed at the root,' he declared to the King. 'I do not care what plots they may hatch against my person,' he added, 'but I cannot stand by while the Queen's life is endangered by a grasping band of immoral foreigners. Madrid is full of Marie Caroline's agents. There are more than two hundred suspect Italians in the capital at this very moment.'

'Have them arrested!' shouted the King tremulously. He could never bear a scene and even less so since his recent illness.

'Even the court is riddled with traitors,' Godoy went on. 'The Countess of Montijo, the Dukes of Villafranca and Montenar — all of them are active members of the treacherous Neapolitan party, led, I regret to say, by your daughter-in-law under her mother's orders.'

'They must be banished,' said the King vehemently. 'And so must the Neapolitan chargé d'affaires, Robertone. I shall send my brother Ferdinand of Naples a firm letter, warning him that we may have to take reprisals against Maria Antoineta.'

'What can we do with that diabolical serpent?' cried the Queen.

In her letters to Godoy she referred to her daughter-in-law variously as 'her mother's spittle', 'a bloodless little animal, all venom and vinegar', 'a half-dead frog', and 'a poisonous viper'.

Godoy informed Napoleon of the subsequent arrests, adding with a great deal of exaggeration:

The Queen of Naples has tried by every means but without success to cause the death of the King and Queen of Spain and mine too. Her instrument is her daughter. Their Majesties are threatened every day with being poisoned. It is up to you, sire, to cause these dangers to cease. The Queen of Naples will endeavour to justify herself. Your Majesty knows her character; there is no need for me to say more.

The Emperor replied melodramatically: 'Nothing surprises me from the Queen of Naples but even so I could not refrain from shuddering when I read your letter.'

To Monsieur de Talleyrand he said: 'Now I can proceed to punish that mischief-maker.' He knew very well that Marie Caroline had a secret agreement with the English in spite of her treaty with France; she flouted this by opening her ports to twelve English and Russian ships carrying 15,000 troops

who, with the aid of the Neapolitans, were to effect a
diversion in Italy while the Emperor was preparing to engage
the German and Prussian armies at Austerlitz. This gave
Napoleon a legitimate excuse to send his troops into the little
kingdom of Naples; they were led by his brother Joseph
whom he appointed King. The banished Neapolitan court
took refuge in Sicily under British protection while in Madrid
the Neapolitan party, following upon the arrests decided by
The Kings, collapsed like a pricked balloon. The split between
the two branches of the Bourbons had served Napoleon's
purpose admirably.

XIV

Godoy was flattered by Napoleon's new friendly attitude to
him. Although he hated the sea and became seasick the
moment he left shore, he determined to become a naval
expert. With the same enthusiasm that he had devoted to
military affairs at the time of the War of the Oranges he now
turned to plans of ships and ports, navigational aids, naval
budgets. He recalled Admiral Gravina from his ambassadorial
post in Paris to command the squadron. Gravina knew about
such tedious details as the exact quantities of cereals required
to make biscuits for sailors at sea and other necessary
supplies about which Godoy was vague. Spain would have a
first-rate navy, modelled on the English one. On 7 February
1805 he wrote to Napoleon: 'I do not see England left on
any map.' The Emperor condescended to call him 'Dear
Cousin' . . .

Naval dreams were soon dispelled. At the end of October
1805 news reached Madrid of the great reverse suffered by
the combined French and Spanish fleet off Trafalgar. Charles
put a brave face on the defeat and sent a medal to Admiral
Gravina who had been wounded in the fray and was dying in
Cadiz. The medal was handed to him upon his deathbed. 'Our

men fought splendidly. They suffered terrible losses before they could be induced to capitulate,' the King told the foreign ambassadors at a gala reception in the palace soon afterwards.

For the Emperor the blow was softened by his subsequent victories on land at Ulm and particularly at Austerlitz against the Austro-Russian forces, but he recognized that British dominance of the sea was beyond dispute. His aide-de-camp Bausset gave an amusing instance of this in his memoirs:

One morning, not long after Austerlitz, the Emperor was working in his study at the palace of St Cloud when Monsieur Denon, the head of his Medals Cabinet, was announced.

'Show him in,' commanded the Emperor crisply, pushing aside the maps he was studying for his projected German campaign.

Monsieur Denon stepped into the study with an obsequious bow. He was a thin, nervous little man with greying hair and beady eyes, over-anxious to please his difficult master whose latest request had been to order a design for three medals to commemorate the victory of Austerlitz. One of these was to be sent to Charles IV.

'Well, Monsieur Denon! have you brought me the medal at last? I was expecting you yesterday,' Napoleon said testily.

Monsieur Denon advanced on tiptoe to the Emperor's desk with an apologetic smile and carefully laid a small silver box upon it with the expectant air of a chef bringing a choice new dish to be sampled by his most fastidious customer.

'I wanted it to be perfect, sire,' he explained, opening the box with a delicate flourish and holding up the medal between his thumb and forefinger for the Emperor's inspection.

'This is the right side,' purred Monsieur Denon.

The Emperor leaned forward and glowered at his effigy.

'H'm. Quite a fair likeness. And the obverse?'

Monsieur Denon turned the medal with a flick of his fingers. The obverse represented an eagle clutching a leopard between its talons.

The Emperor looked puzzled. 'What is that supposed to signify?'

Monsieur Denon's smile broadened. He was evidently pleased with his invention. 'It represents the eagle of France strangling the English leopard, sire, the leopard – as you know – being one of the attributes of . . .'

Before he could complete his sentence Napoleon had snatched the medal from his hands and flung it to the far end of the room.

'Vile flatterer!' he shouted, rising to confront the astonished Monsieur Denon. 'Vile flatterer! How dare you suggest that the French eagle is strangling the English leopard? I cannot put a miserable fishing boat out to sea without its being captured by the English. It is the leopard that is strangling the French eagle. Have this medal melted down immediately and never dare to show me anything so absurd again.'

'I beg your pardon, sire, I never intended - '

'Get out!' thundered the Emperor.

Monsieur Denon hurriedly picked up the silver box from the table and the slighted medal from the floor and scuttled speedily away.

XV

Weakened by two miscarriages the consumptive little Princess Maria Antoineta fell into a decline and died in May 1806. It was rumoured that her mother-in-law had poisoned her but, dearly as the various members of the Bourbon family would no doubt have liked to poison each other and made frequent use of the word 'poison' in their correspondence, there is no evidence that Maria Luisa resorted to such an extremity; she did not need to.

Doctors Marcelo Sanchez and Pedro Castello wrote and

duly signed a report on the Princess's illness including such details as the weight of the pus she had expectorated daily before her death. The Queen had as usual kept Godoy informed by daily bulletins. She told him that every kind of medicine was tried to cure the Princess, 'even Neapolitan remedies suggested by Maria Antoineta herself, such as vipers' broth'; the Queen supplied statistics of her evacuations, expectorations, fevers, her insatiable thirst, her compulsive desire to eat lettuce seasoned with pure vinegar and highly-seasoned truffled omelettes. The doctor's autopsy revealed that the Princess had a large heart, dilated ventricules, scirrhosis of the lungs, tubercular calcifications, a small stomach and an abdomen full of pus. Her body was covered with spots.

When Napoleon was informed of the Princess's death he ordered a black crêpe armband and murmured reflectively: 'she will have to be replaced.'

Godoy made a final bid for Ferdinand's friendship, or subjection, by proposing that the Prince should marry his sister-in-law Maria Luisa de Bourbon y Villabriga. When this suggestion was put before him Ferdinand is said to have replied: 'I would prefer to remain a widower all my life, or to become a monk, than become Godoy's brother-in-law!' (In fact he married again three times after he became King.)

The Prince's movements continued to be closely observed; he was suspected by The Kings and Godoy of hatching a plot against the favourite. A lecherous priest, Father Martras, who had been dismissed from the Prince's household, denounced several palace servants, including the barber Antonio Moreno, who was asked why he stayed so long alone with the Prince. Moreno replied that it was in order to assist at the chemistry experiments in which it was well known that Ferdinand took an interest. This obscure affair was dealt with *in camera*; mysterious allusions were made to letters alleged to have shown disrespect to Their Majesties and, by order of the King, four of the Prince's servants were sentenced to exile in South America: Moreno the barber; Zacarias Garcia, an accountant;

Saturnino de Segovia, a furniture-mover; and Fernin de Artieda, a 'common valet'. These men, however, could not sail either from Cadiz or Corunna because of the blockade of these ports by British ships so they were imprisoned at Corunna until Ferdinand's accession to the throne.

Don Antonio, the Prince's uncle, was one of his confidants and Godoy must have advised the Queen to warn him, for she wrote to the favourite 'all that you have counselled Antonio is very sound but I doubt whether he will follow it because he is stupid and therefore obstinate, with bad advisers: country people and low servants.'

Godoy felt that he should take precautions. He had himself appointed Inspector of the King's military household, so as to secure control of all that went on inside the palace. Ferdinand's friend the Duke of San Carlos was made viceroy of the semi-independent province of Navarre and replaced by a friend of Godoy whose brother, Don Diego, Duke of Almodovar, was put in charge of the palace guards. Godoy increased the number of hussars who guarded his own palace of Buenavista to fifty. In addition to these fifty grenadier guards, three officers, fifty-six artillerymen and two cannons were scattered throughout his palace grounds.

Napoleon's postponement of his 'Portuguese plan' was a further source of concern to the favourite. In reply to his letter, transmitted by Izquierdo, in which he stated unequivocally:

My security rests on the Emperor's protection. I may survive that misfortune, the death of my sovereigns, but before that terrible moment comes I am bound to assure myself of an existence out of the reach of violence . . .

the Emperor had, upon Talleyrand's advice, asked for more precise details. Cornered, Godoy finally suggested in black and white that Portugal should be cut up into four portions: two for himself and the Infante Francisco de Paula, one for the Infante Don Carlos and the fourth for the Portuguese Regent. By committing himself thus in writing Godoy put himself squarely into Napoleon's hands.

But the Emperor was in no hurry to take action. More important problems claimed his attention in western and central Europe and he preferred to solve them one by one. 'The time has not yet come,' he replied evasively, 'to deal with Portugal. Each event has its prescribed hour. They follow one another in a sequence that cannot be precipitated or altered without endangering their outcome.'

The English government was aware that Portugal formed the subject of correspondence between France and Spain, but did the British cabinet really believe that the country was seriously threatened, and that the occupation of Lisbon would provide a guarantee against an invasion? In any event, on 24 July 1806 the decision was taken to send a squadron to the Tagus and on 14 August six ships with nine battalions on board entered the port of Lisbon proclaiming that they had come 'to defend Portugal against an impending attack by the French and Spanish'. The English commander, St Vincent, rented a house in town as if to prove that he intended to settle down there. Banquets were held on board and toasts drunk to 'the floating walls of Britain lined up in front of the walls of Lisbon'. Rosslyn, the army commander, sent a note to the Regent offering to send 10,000 men for the defence of Portugal. Talleyrand got wind of this and protested energetically while the Portuguese plaintively declared that all they wanted was peace to enable them to restore their finances.

Godoy turned and twisted, unable to decide which side to favour. He made an attempt to cultivate the friendship of General Murat, Napoleon's brother-in-law, in the mistaken belief that he had influence with the Emperor. 'There are many similarities in our characters and hearts,' Godoy wrote to Murat, to whom he sent a gift of horses and merino sheep. Murat impudently asked for the Order of the Golden Fleece and his request was graciously granted.

In addition to Portugal, England was taking an active interest in South America. Buenos Aires was briefly captured in September 1806. Would it then be wise for Spain to ally herself with England? Godoy formed a project — not devoid of good sense — for a triple alliance of Russia, England and Spain, with the Americas, against France. He suggested making a separate peace with England and this idea was sent to London through the Russian ambassador Strogonoff; but it met with a cold reception by Pitt, who believed that such a scheme would expose Spain to a spontaneous invasion by France and the country was too weak to offer any resistance. British aid would only be forthcoming if Spain was to declare herself firmly against France and adhere to the coalition. Lord Yarmouth, the English ambassador in Paris, asked Izquierdo what Spain's peace conditions would be; Izquierdo, thinking that this was a trap set by Talleyrand, replied: 'Trinidad and Gibraltar.' It was not the first time that such conditions had been mooted, but Yarmouth replied flatly that no English minister would ever be a party to the cession of Gibraltar and that he did not want to die stoned in the streets of London by an angry populace. So that was that.

In view of this rebuff, what could have prompted Godoy to publish, on 6 October 1806, the extraordinary manifesto which, although it did not mention France by name, was taken by the public — and others — to refer explicitly to that country? This 'very singular document', as Lord Strangford, the British ambassador in Lisbon, described it, was a call to arms against an unnamed foe. The Spanish people were urgently requested to contribute horses, fodder, monetary donations and assistance 'in view of the present dangerous situation'. At the same time a circular was sent to the governors of provinces referring to 'the war which we may be forced to wage for the general welfare'. These orders, issued at a time when the French army was occupied on the Rhine, were a stab in the back of Spain's ally, France. Since they could not possibly be implemented, they amounted to no more than a wasp's sting whose only consequence was to inflame Napoleon and make him more distrustful than ever of the favourite.

The Kings bestowed a final title upon him, that of 'Most

Serene Highness', which the new French ambassador, the Marquis of Beauharnais (Josephine's brother-in-law), who reached Madrid in December 1806, ostensibly ignored, thus provoking Godoy still further.

The circular to the provincial governors was dated 14 October 1806; an unfortunate choice, for on that same day Napoleon won a great victory at Jena, followed by his triumphal entry into Berlin. Godoy's manifesto was hastily shelved.

The Spanish sovereigns were so shattered by the news of Napoleon's progress that a foreign ambassador reported soon afterwards: 'At the last gala held at the palace Charles IV was so distraught that he had to retire early and the Queen was so agitated that she spoke in Italian to the French ambassador and in French to the Italian.' She confided to Godoy: 'The French make me feel so uneasy,' and Charles, in a rare flash of prescience, exclaimed mournfully: 'Our turn will come and we shall be the last victims if the Emperor Alexander of Russia does not succeed in conquering the French colossus.' Seven months later Napoleon concluded the Peace of Tilsit with Alexander.

Almost at the same moment Napoleon observed to Prince Metternich in Berlin: 'The members of the Spanish royal house are my personal enemies; they and I cannot sit on thrones at the same time.' The Emperor convened the Portuguese envoy Pardo de Figueroa and during their discussion the subject of Spain was raised. Charles had recently been ill again and Napoleon began by expressing the hope that he was in a better state of health, for he was sure, he said, that the King of Spain would always be his faithful ally. 'I would not believe in the authenticity of his signature at the bottom of a hostile missive,' he assured Figueroa. 'I firmly believe in his friendship. But there is a worm in it. There is a certain distrust of me at the Spanish court. The English are responsible for this. I know what they are up to and the instrument they have found in the heir to the throne. I doubt, however, whether Godoy, whom the latter detests, would consent and sacrifice his country to England.'

But when Figueroa, in an attempt to defend Godoy, said that he was a friend of France, Napoleon sharply rejoined: 'Have you read his proclamation? Do you know that he has armed the country on the pretext of the presence of an English squadron in Lisbon? English forces are being assembled at Falmouth . . . expeditions are under way under the command of Sir Arthur Wellesley and Sir George Provost. It is said that I wish to dethrone the Bourbons to give the crown to a member of my family. If I did so, what would my allies think? What surety could they have in my alliance for the future? If I wounded the feelings of a people whose national pride is well known to me, why should I plunge into an adventure which would oblige me to turn my attention from the northern powers where my enemies are? I am Spain's friend from a sense of duty, for sentimental reasons and in my own interest. I believe, Mr Ambassador, that I have explained myself frankly, have I not? The day I want it to do so, the hostile faction in Spain will cross over to my side. I rely upon Spain to bring Portugal over to my policy by reason or by force.'

Napoleon wished Spain to give him a tangible proof of her friendly sentiments and to this end she was invited, on 29 December 1806, to adhere to the blockade decreed in Berlin in November. At first Godoy hesitated. Among other drawbacks, there was a considerable trade in wine, fruit and wool between Britain and Spain in which he had a personal stake. In January 1807, however, he succumbed. Much publicity was given to his order to have all English books stocked by Madrid shops publicly burned. This was followed by a decree forbidding trade with Britain. Talleyrand ordered Beauharnais to ask for 4,000 cavalry men and 10,000 soldiers to be sent to Hanover to oppose the English army which was said to be about to disembark there and force the blockade. On 3 January 1807 Godoy formally announced that Charles had put 14,000 men at the disposal of his ally, but as usual Spanish preparations proceeded at a slow pace.

After the conclusion of the Peace of Tilsit with the Emperor Alexander Napoleon felt free to devote his attention to his arch-enemy England. Talleyrand was asked to invite Portugal to close her ports to the English – the perennial demand. If she refused to do so by 1 September she would be occupied by a Franco-Spanish army. After a ten months' absence, the Emperor returned to France on 27 July 1807 and began to organize an expeditionary force of 30,000 men at Bayonne.

Lord Strangford warned the Porguguese Regent that French troops were en route, but England refused to send any help to Portugal. She merely urged that unfortunate country to make efforts to help herself. George III, however, wrote a personal letter thanking the Regent for respecting British citizens and their property. On the other hand, Foreign Secretary Canning was ready to occupy Madeira on the pretext of holding it for Portugal. A secret convention was signed on 12 September 1807 between Canning and Sousa Coutinho by which it was agreed that the Governor of Madeira would make a token resistance against the English for the sake of form. The treaty envisaged the opening of Brazilian ports to English ships. The Regent was advised to embark for that country as a last resort in the event of an invasion of his country.

PART FOUR

THE ESCORIAL AFFAIR

XVI

Napoleon had told Figueroa in Berlin that the enemy Spanish
faction would go over to his side whenever he wanted it to,
and his words came true sooner than he had anticipated. In
the summer of 1807, Ferdinand and his friends, particularly
Canon Escoiquiz, were pressing him to seek Napoleon's
support by marrying into his family. Canon Escoiquiz wrote
in his memoirs that Beauharnais's predecessor had observed
to Godoy at a reception given by the French embassy that if
the Prince did not marry a princess of imperial blood Spain
would be exposed to the risk of an invasion. This remark was
overheard by a gentleman called Pascual Vallejo who,
according to Escoiquiz, was a diplomat well connected with
foreign embassies.

Ferdinand told Escoiquiz on 17 June 1807 that a member
of the French embassy had approached persons of his
household, Juan Manuel de Villena and Brigadier Pedro
Giraldo, to tell them confidentially that 'the French ambassador wished to have a private interview with His Royal
Highness about a matter of some importance.' The Prince
asked the Canon for his advice and in the meantime let it be
known to the French that he 'appreciated this mark of the
Emperor's goodwill. It was, however, impossible for him to
speak to the ambassador alone.'

Escoiquiz then offered to act as intermediary through the
Duke of Infantado. The latter was to suggest to the
ambassador that Escoiquiz wished to present him with a copy
of his poem on the Conquest of Mexico with a view to its
translation and publication in French.

The Canon duly called upon Beauharnais with two copies
of his mediocre poem. One of them was intended for the
French Institute – no doubt he hoped to pass to posterity as
an *homme de lettres.*

As soon as he had told the ambassador in a confidential

aside that he had a message for him from Ferdinand, Beauharnais led him into an inner room. The Canon then asked whether it was true that Beauharnais had received a message from the Emperor; the ambassador denied this but Escoiquiz added, 'he did not inquire who had led us to believe that a message had been received' and he therefore deduced, probably mistakenly, that there had been some correspondence on the subject. Beauharnais, according to the Canon, went so far as to assure him that he would be pleased to have relations with Ferdinand and that this would also please the Emperor.

No more was said until a further meeting took place some days later in the gardens of the Retiro, in the middle of the afternoon, at a time when most people were taking a siesta. In the meanwhile the Marquis of Beauharnais had written to Champagny, the French Minister of Foreign Affairs who had replaced Talleyrand (promoted to the rank of Grand Chamberlain of the Emperor's palace), for guidance. The Retiro gardens of Madrid were attached to a palace built in the grounds of a monastery where the former Kings of Spain withdrew for a spiritual retreat during Holy Week and in times of mourning. It had now changed its religious character and become more mundane. Philip II gave nautical fêtes on the lake before he sank into his gloomy Escorial contemplative phase. Godoy had recently made alterations to the theatre in the royal park without consulting the King; for once in his life Charles had disapproved and been peeved with the favourite.

Canon Escoiquiz strolled by the lakeside pretending to be engrossed in the *Madrid Gazette,* as had previously been arranged. In spite of the August heat he had stuck on his false black beard to avoid being recognized. The Canon was now about to give free rein to his love of intrigue and to play the leading role he had coveted for so long, after nearly seven years in the wilderness of Toledo. At 2.30 p.m. two figures sauntered through the iron-wrought gates below the esplanade: the French ambassador and his colleague Monsieur

Gasset. The three men greeted each other then walked along the edge of the lake like friends engaged in casual conversation, the Canon darting a sharp and practised eye from time to time towards the shrubberies to make sure they had not been followed. Pepita Tudó's residence overlooked the Retiro — one had to be constantly on the alert. The Marquis waited for the Canon to speak first since it was he who had solicited the interview to carry matters a step farther.

'Your Excellency,' Escoiquiz began, 'you are no doubt aware of the difficult situation in which the Prince of Asturias finds himself? The Prince is virtually a prisoner and is debarred from the society of any person to whom he shows friendship. I — his ex-tutor — have been banished from court for a number of years. The latest banishment is that of the Duke of San Carlos who has been replaced at the palace by a spy in the pay of Manuel Godoy. And yet this man Godoy has had the effrontery to suggest that the Prince should marry his wife's sister! The Kings, particularly the Queen, are entirely under Godoy's thumb. Both the Queen and her favourite are capable of the most dastardly schemes. The King is weak and ailing. What will happen to the Prince of Asturias when he dies? It is a matter of the utmost concern to all his friends and supporters. The people are loyal to him but what could they do if, say, an accident occurred to the heir to the throne brought about by devious means? On the other hand, the Prince must remarry and produce an heir. He is a sincere admirer of the Emperor Napoleon and will be his staunchest ally the day he assumes the crown of Spain and the Indies. Would it not be possible, Your Excellency, to find a bride for him in the Emperor's family?'

'Has the Prince of Asturias actually expressed this wish himself?' asked the Marquis.

'He has, Your Excellency; that is the sole reason for my present approach. The Prince has empowered me to ask you for your opinion on this subject and to convey his sentiments of loyalty and devotion to the Emperor.'

The Marquis hesitated before replying: 'You understand,

Canon, that you are placing me in a very delicate position. As the official representative of His Imperial Majesty I have no authority to enter into what could be termed backdoor negotiations.'

As the Canon raised his hands in protest, Beauharnais went on: 'Nevertheless, I fully realize that the circumstances are out of the ordinary; believe me when I say that the Prince of Asturias has my deepest sympathy. I am prepared to take the risk of helping him as far as it is in my power to do so. But I must have the Prince's personal assurance that he desires me to send word to the Emperor. It is not that I doubt your word, Canon, not for a moment, but a guarantee is imperative. The Emperor is bound to insist upon it.'

'I thank you, Your Excellency, for your expression of interest and sympathy. I am most grateful,' the Canon replied. 'I fully understand that you wish for a confirmation from the Prince before proceeding further. We anticipated that such would be the case. Since it is impossible for you to engage in a private conversation with His Royal Highness without being overheard, we shall have to resort to a harmless little stratagem – such as an agreed signal or exchange of words at a palace reception – after which we two could, if you agree, arrange another meeting to discuss the details of an official approach to the Emperor.'

The Canon, an expert on the subject of codes and secret messages, had already thought up a plan which he confided to the ambassador.

The Marquis wrote again to Champagny. The only available French princess appeared to be Napoleon's niece, Lucien's daughter Charlotte. Alternatively, there was Josephine's cousin, Mademoiselle Marie Tascher de la Pagerie ...

XVII

The elaborate crystal chandeliers from the royal glass manufacture of La Granja were ablaze with light in the reception rooms of the palace where grandees and foreign diplomats were attending the last levee of the season before the court left for San Lorenzo.

The King, who was suffering from rheumatism in the knees, found it difficult to repress both his pain and his boredom. Maria Luisa, dressed in her favourite yellow, with her diamond arrow and a garland of yellow roses in her hair, prattled vivaciously. His Most Serene Highness Manuel Godoy was also in a good humour, for at long last his Portuguese plan was appearing to take shape. Napoleon was actually doing something about it and a secret treaty between France and Spain was being discussed in Paris. The Emperor had urged Spain, once more, to put pressure on Portugal and back up his demands to close ports to English vessels and to confiscate British goods. If the court of Lisbon proved recalcitrant Spain was invited to join France in the conquest of Portugal. Godoy was delighted; the Emperor had evidently forgiven him for the threatening manifesto he had published the year before.

Izquierdo reported in a confidential dispatch that in Napoleon's opinion it would be advisable to make the King of Spain suzerain over Portugal, to apportion part of the Kingdom to Godoy and another to Luisetta, Queen of Etruria (a kingdom which Napoleon had long desired to annex, all the more so now that nearly the whole of Italy belonged to him). In the Emperor's view, the conquest of Portugal could be made to serve several of his designs: it would help him in his blockade against England; it would enable him to send his troops into Etruria, and it would bring him several steps nearer the objective which he had mentioned to Metternich — the elimination of the Spanish

Bourbons. The Spanish Kings, blind to the danger, were eagerly anticipating the secret convention due to be signed at Fontainebleau in the autumn.

Godoy, under the delusion that he would soon achieve the climax of his brilliant career by having a crown placed upon his head, passed smilingly among the guests at the levee. Ferdinand surprised everybody by looking as if he too were enjoying himself. Since the death of his wife he eagerly sought out all visitors to the palace, particularly foreigners, to make up for the lack of conversation and social relationships in his monotonous life.

The Marquis of Beauharnais approached the Queen, kissed her beringed hand with a low bow, and paid her a compliment which made her beam with unfeigned pleasure. Then she asked him about the health of his sister-in-law, the Empress Josephine, whom she was destined to meet in less than a year. The Marquis turned to speak to the King on the subject of the chase, one of the few topics which brought some glimmer of life and interest to that sovereign's placid face. Finally, he paused briefly before the Prince of Asturias.

'Have you ever been to Naples, Your Excellency?' the Prince asked him, taking a handkerchief from his pocket.

This was the agreed 'signal'.

'Indeed I have, it is a beautiful city,' replied the Marquis; he continued to expatiate upon the subject. The two men exchanged significant glances, the Prince turned to blow his nose and the Marquis passed on. Now he knew that Ferdinand wished him to continue his discussions with Escoiquiz.

That evening the Canon had another clandestine meeting with Beauharnais who showed him Champagny's reply to his first letter. The Minister wanted the Prince of Asturias to put his proposal to the Emperor in writing. This seemed to imply that Champagny had spoken to him and that it was Napoleon who had insisted upon a written confirmation, as he had done when Godoy first approached him about the partition of Portugal.

'It would be better if the letter were to be written in French. Could you help me to draft it?' asked the Canon. 'Then I will place it before the Prince for his signature.'

The Marquis agreed and two days later the Canon translated the draft letter to Ferdinand, whose knowledge of French, as of most other subjects, was sketchy. The Prince, however, did not sign the letter until he had had the opportunity of showing it to his close friends, particularly the Duke of Infantado and the Duke of Montijo.

The court left La Granja on 22 September to take up residence at San Lorenzo, or the Escorial, which Ferdinand held in particular aversion since the death of Maria Antoineta, for the supposed part it had played in his domestic tragedy. He was housed, at his request, in the prior's apartments next to the monastery, which he had occupied in his bachelor days. It had turned cold early and the winds whistled through the long passages; the shivering halberdiers gathered round the braziers whenever their stringent duties allowed them a few minutes' respite. Among them were Godoy's spies, who reported on the unusual activity being displayed by the Prince, mysterious comings and goings to his apartments, the visits of Canon Escoiquiz, to whom, on 11 October, the Prince finally entrusted the letter addressed to Napoleon.

Sire [he wrote] I consider this day as the happiest in my life seeing that it affords me the opportunity of expressing to Your Imperial Majesty, to a hero destined by Providence to restore peace, order and prosperity in Europe, threatened as it is by a complete overthrow, and to strengthen tottering thrones, the sentiments of admiration and respect with which your brilliant qualities inspire me. I should have had, a long time since, this satisfaction, as well as that of assuring Your Imperial Majesty of the sincere desire which I have to see the existing friendship between our two houses and the alliance between our two nations, become closer every day, by means of a marriage which would unite me to a Princess of Your Majesty's family. But circumstances have obliged me to be silent, and it is only in consequence of the explanation of Monsieur de Beauharnais and of the information which he has given me as to the wishes of Your Imperial Majesty that I have resolved to speak . . . I fear that this step, so innocent in the terms in which I make it, and in the position I am in, might be construed as a crime should it be discovered.

Your Imperial Majesty knows much better than I that the best Kings are the most exposed to become victims of the artifices of the ambitious and intriguing men who surround them. Our court is not free from such men and the benevolence and uprightness of my dear parents expose them the more to be the victims of unloyal plots. I fear that those men may have obtained their consent to some other projected marriage for me, more suitable to their own interests, and I take the liberty of asking Your Majesty to open the eyes of my dear parents and to get them to adopt the alliance which I ask of you.

As for myself, full of respect and filial obedience towards my parents, I can only play a passive part in this matter and this will be to refuse any alliance which shall not have the approval of Your Majesty.

Ferdinand's letter reached Fontainebleau on the morning of 27 October, a few hours before the signing of the secret Treaty of Fountainebleau between France and Spain.

Napoleon did not wait for the treaty to be signed before taking action. On 12 October he sent orders to General Junot, the commander of the forces massed at Bayonne, a few miles from the Spanish frontier, to start at once for Lisbon 'so as to forestall the English', and Champagny sent a letter to Charles on the same day asking him to show the greatest energy in the war which was about to be launched. In a dramatic scene enacted before the entire diplomatic court assembled at Fontainebleau on 14 October, Napoleon declared to the Portuguese ambassador, loud enough for all present to hear: 'I shall declare war on every power that has a British ambassador or minister.'

The Portuguese Regent, who promised to close his ports to the English on 20 September, asked for the French march to be stopped. Eighty-two English ships left Lisbon under the protection of a frigate taking off British citizens and their effects; those of Oporto, filled to the brim with furniture and barrels of port, left in sixty ships escorted by two frigates. An embargo was placed on British ships in the Tagus. Lord Strangford asked for his passport.

Junot crossed the Bidassoa, the narrow river separating France and Spain, on 19 October; he and his men received a warm welcome from the still unsuspecting Spaniards who treated them as allies, but heavy rains and rough mountain tracks impeded his progress. Of the Spanish troops who accompanied him, 1,700 perished from hunger, sickness or drowning in the torrents. 'Press on,' Napoleon repeatedly urged Junot. 'Lisbon is all important. You must get there as soon as possible to confiscate English property and goods. Appear in the guise of friends, but seize the Portuguese fleet.'

Junot pressed on doggedly, anxious to restore himself in the Emperor's good graces; he had been under a cloud since Napoleon had discovered his affair with his sister Caroline, who was married to General Murat, Grand Duke of Berg.

XVIII

Seated round the conference table at Fontainebleau, the French delegates and Izquierdo (the Spanish ambassador knew nothing about these negotiations) drafted the clauses of the treaty designed to dismember their western neighbour. It was agreed that the little King of Etruria, through his mother Maria Luisa (Luisetta), should cede that kingdom to France in exchange for the Portuguese province of Entre Minho e Douro, with the title of King of Northern Lusitania. A larger slice of territory, comprising the Algarve and Alemtejo, was earmarked for Godoy although Napoleon probably guessed that 'unforeseen events' – upon which he relied so heavily – would prevent the favourite from ever taking possession of this kingdom.

The regions in between were not to be definitely disposed of until the general peace was declared. Charles IV received the title of 'Protector of the province of Entre Minho e Douro', the hollow title of 'Emperor of the Two Americas', and Napoleon guaranteed the integrity of the Spanish territory south of the Pyrenees.

A separate military convention sanctioned the entry into

Spain of the French troops already marching against Lisbon, with the help of 11,000 Spanish soldiers, and 16,000 more were to invade the north and south of Portugal. A further French corps of 40,000 men was to assemble at Bayonne to support the first in the event of a British attack, but its entry into Spain would not take place without prior consultation between the two contracting powers. In brief, the greater part of Spain's trained forces were to be engaged in Portugal while Napoleon was preparing to flood the peninsula with his own troops.

To cap it all came the grovelling letter from the Prince of Asturias asking for Napoleon's protection. What should he do with Ferdinand? What kind of a young man was he? What kind of a man could he be, this offspring of a dull-witted father and a lustful, hysterical mother? Would it be a good idea to bring him into the Napoleonic family circle? 'I only want relatives who can be of use to me,' the Emperor had once declared. Once again he decided to play for time, to wait for some external event which would help him to reach a decision. As it happened, a momentous event was taking place at that very moment within the granite walls of the Escorial.

On 27 October Charles found a slip of paper on his study table whose contents were enough to bring on another attack of apoplexy — so much so that one may speculate whether this had been the intention of the anonymous writer, or of the person who had dictated the note. It read:

Prince Ferdinand is preparing an uprising in the palace; your crown is in danger. The Queen risks being poisoned [again!]. It is urgent to prevent this at all costs. The faithful subject who gives you this warning is not in a position to fulfil his duties in any other manner.

Godoy was absent from San Lorenzo on the day of this denunciation. He was kept in Madrid by an alleged heavy cold accompanied by a high fever; he went to the length of making his two personal physicians sign a certificate to this effect. It is difficult to believe that he had no part in the discovery of the 'plot', if he was not the actual author of the warning note. He had been feeling so discouraged latterly that he had written to Izquierdo (early in October): 'I would like to put an end to my career, but I need a general peace for that.'

As soon as the King had read the anonymous note he showed it to the Queen. She, too, one suspects, must have known about it beforehand. The Kings, full of righteous wrath, repaired immediately to Ferdinand's room on the pretext of presenting him with a richly-bound volume on the Spanish American conquests (this is Canon Escoiquiz's version of the story; others differ slightly from the following account, but not in essence).

Ferdinand showed such fear and astonishment when his parents appeared that the King was sure he was hiding something from them. The Prince's eyes turned to the bureau where he kept his private papers. The King asked for the key; this was produced after much fumbling. Charles opened the drawers one by one and removed a sheaf of documents. 'What are they?' he asked. Ferdinand declined to give an explanation. He began to stammer and then relapsed into his customary silence before his parents.

'Very well, since you refuse to reply you will be detained in your room until we have read these papers,' the King decreed.

When the Duke of Ayerbe, who belonged to the Prince's household, called upon him a little before supper that evening, Ferdinand gave him two missives to be delivered at once by trustworthy messengers. One was addressed to the Duke of Infantado (who had left the capital to visit ailing relatives in northern Spain). The other was for Canon Escoiquiz in Toledo.

Two days later, at 4 p.m. on 29 October, the Canon was informed by his old housekeeper that a traveller from Cuenca had galloped up to his little house near the cathedral with an urgent message. The Canon asked her to show the stranger in.

Before he had time to ask for his identity the stranger

boldly asked him whether he was in fact before Canon Escoiquiz. Not satisfied with the latter's assurance, he demanded a confirmation by producing a copy of the famous 'Conquest of Mexico' and asked the the bewildered Canon to recite the first stanzas of his own composition. It was only after he had passed this test, devised by Ferdinand, that the stranger handed him the Prince's letter:

Friend Escoiquiz, last night my parents took possession of all my papers, among them the keys to the code we have used in our correspondence, the note against the Prince of the Peace and your reply to me about the message received from the French embassy. I am writing this to warn you. Please advise me what I should do. 28 October, the Escorial.

The Canon quickly wrote a reply to the Prince, counselling him to answer all interrogations 'with dignity and nobility' and to assure everybody that he had done nothing wrong. The messenger left Toledo immediately but by the time he got back to the Escorial the Prince had been imprisoned and the message could not be delivered.

As soon as the messenger had left, the Canon, correctly guessing that he would soon be arrested, arranged for the two relatives who shared his house to pack and leave for the neighbouring village of Burguillos so as not to be incriminated. He then waited for the inevitable royal command.

At the Escorial, events moved at a melodramatic pace. On the evening of 27 October Charles and Maria Luisa eagerly scanned the papers they had retrieved from their son's bureau. These included a lengthy expository letter written by Escoiquiz and signed by Ferdinand, directed against Godoy and denouncing the scandals associated with him: how he had 'prostituted the flower of Spain's womanhood from the highest to the lowest classes in his private audiences; how Godoy prevented The Kings from meeting the most eminent men in the country and wished to dominate The Kings and the Prince by appointing his friends to be their confessors. Godoy was said to be responsible for the scant esteem in which the Prince was held by his parents and for the isolation in which he lived. The plan to marry him to Godoy's sister-in-law was a means of his getting closer to the throne and spying upon the Prince. Godoy was in league with France through his secret agent Izquierdo and plotting against his masters. The Prince concluded by asking for a private conversation with his father, preferably during a hunt, to ensure privacy, in the course of which he would adduce evidence of his accusations. He advised the King to have both Godoy and his mistress Pepita Tudó thrown into prison.'

The effect produced upon The Kings by this tirade against their beloved favourite may be imagined. Their fury blinded them to such an extent that they took the next document they happened to pick up to be a warrant for the King's assassination. In fact it was a draft (similar to the document discussed in Maria Antoineta's lifetime) in the form of a decree (rather prematurely sealed with black wax) intended for publication by Ferdinand in the event of his father's death and by which he appointed the Duke of Infantado Captain General of New Castile, empowering him to arrest any person who might oppose Ferdinand's ascent to the throne. It was a measure directed against the possible machinations of Godoy to seize power.

The other papers, as Ferdinand had warned the Canon, included the key to the cypher used between them in their correspondence and various notes which The Kings, in their excitement and agitation, do not appear to have read carefully at that moment. They interrupted the reading to write to Godoy for his advice, to summon the Minister of Grace and Justice, Caballero, and the governor of the Council of Castile, Señor Arias, to San Lorenzo. These two gentlemen arrived at the palace at 6 p.m. on 29 October.

In his memoirs Godoy writes that he advised The Kings to be prudent and appeal to the judiciary only as a last resort. Caballero was not one of his friends. Nevertheless, it is difficult to accept that The Kings, who never acted upon their own initiative, would have taken such an energetic step without the approval of the man whose projected downfall was the mainspring of the Prince's alleged 'plot'.

This was not the first time that a judge had been asked to investigate the Prince's motives and actions, but whereas in the previous instance only the Prince's servants had been questioned and the proceedings held *in camera*, now the blame was put firmly and publicly upon Ferdinand's shoulders. This was an altogether more serious attempt to discredit the heir to the throne. He was asked to appear before a solemn tribunal composed of his parents, Caballero and Arias, with every intention of having the facts spread abroad.

In view of the fairly innocuous nature of the documents discovered in the Prince's apartments, it is difficult to understand why the King should have written so hastily to Napoleon to acquaint him with the events of the Escorial, and this was before the interrogations had been completed. Was it because The Kings, and Godoy, were afraid of the possible effects upon the implementation of the Treaty of Fontainebleau? This treaty was actually signed on the day the anonymous note was delivered to Charles. Was it a move inspired by Godoy to alienate Ferdinand from the Emperor and prove how unworthy an heir he was? In this case Godoy could not have been aware of Ferdinand's relations with the French ambassador.

Emotion, not reason, dictated the extraordinary letter which Charles addressed to Napoleon on 29 October.

Monsieur my Brother, at a time when my thoughts were concentrated upon the best means of contributing to the destruction of our mutual enemy, when I believed that the conspiracies of the ex-Queen of Naples had been buried with her daughter, I learn with a horror that makes me shudder that the most appalling intrigue was being hatched in my palace. My heart bleeds to relate such a terrible event! My eldest son, heir presumptive to my throne, had plotted to dethrone me, had even contemplated an attack against his mother. Such a dreadful plot must be punished with all the rigour of the law. The law of succession must be revoked; one of his brothers will be more worthy to replace him in my heart and on the throne. I am at the moment looking for his accomplices to find out more about this dark deed but I do not wish to delay for a moment informing Your Imperial Majesty and I beg you to assist me with your counsels . . .

The above was written after the first interrogation on 29 October during which Ferdinand had stalled and hardly uttered a word. During the second interrogation on the following day, however, he broke down completely. The Queen recounted the scene to Lord and Lady Holland after her own fashion during her subsequent exile in Rome.

'Well sir, what is the meaning of this tirade against Manuel Godoy?' Charles demanded, picking up the memorandum written by Escoiquiz to be used as the basis of a confidential talk between father and son in an attempt to 'open the King's eyes' to what was going on around him.

'It is a monstrous document,' the Queen exploded. 'A tissue of lies – infamous lies. Who helped you to write it, Ferdinand? The style is not yours. You would not be capable of composing such a long piece of prose.'

'It – it was written by Maria Antoineta a long time ago,' Ferdinand blurted impulsively.

'You are lying, Ferdinand, you are lying,' the King shouted. 'In this document Godoy is referred to by the initials H.S.H., His Serene Highness – a title which was not bestowed upon him during the lifetime of your late wife.'

The Prince lowered his head and remained silent.

'What have you got to say, sir – answer me!' Charles bellowed.

Ferdinand still refused to answer.

'And this,' added the Queen, waving a sheet of paper before his face, 'this key to a cypher. What plot is this?'

'It is not a plot – only a cypher . . .'

'To whom does your Royal Highness write in it?' asked Caballero.

Ferdinand blew his nose and said nothing.

'And this decree, sealed in black,' the King went on, 'which refers to my death . . .'

'I – I was only taking precautions,' Ferdinand mumbled.

'Precautions? What do you mean?' the Queen asked him sharply.

'Should – should anything happen to my father, which

God forbid, I would have no support; worse, I would very probably be ousted from the throne.'

'Your actions prove how little you deserve one,' the Queen observed.

'S-so,' Ferdinand went on quickly, 'I deemed it advisable to make sure there would be no trouble when I ascend the throne, which is my right.'

'A most unsatisfactory explanation,' said the King.

'And these notes – what are they about?' asked the Queen, picking up the paper on which the Prince had written, in cryptic sentences, the gist of his own draft letter to Napoleon about his proposed marriage with a French princess. The Prince was paying dearly for his carelessness; the Canon had strongly advised him to burn these notes.

'Those,' he stammered, becoming confused, 'were used for the draft of a letter to the Emperor Napoleon asking him for the hand of a member of his family. I don't want to be married to Godoy's sister-in-law.'

'But this is heinous!' exclaimed the Queen. 'You have plotted behind our backs with our ally Napoleon? You have disgraced yourself and us. When was this letter sent?'

'On . . . on 12 October,' said Ferdinand weakly.

'You will pay for this, Ferdinand. God will not allow such wickedness to go unpunished,' said the King piously.

'I have done nothing by myself . . . I was wrongly advised,' lubbered Ferdinand.

'Who advised you?' Charles asked him.

Ferdinand shook his head miserably.

'We command you as your parents and sovereigns: who advised you?' the Queen demanded.

'It is important,' Caballero insisted, 'that you should tell us who led you astray, Your Royal Highness. It is in your own interest – it will diminish your responsibility.'

Ferdinand crumbled under this combined assault; he could also see that it was a possible way out. 'The Duke of Infantado suggested the draft decree; the letter to the Emperor was written by Canon Escoiquiz and the French ambassador.'

'The French ambassador?' cried Charles. 'Has he been a party to this? Take care what you say. This is very serious.'

'It is true. I swear.'

The Prince then blurted out the names of all his friends and advisers: the Dukes of San Carlos, Hijar, Montijo, Chaves, Bornos, the Marquis of Ayerbe ...

'They shall be dealt with, and so will you, sir. This terrible affair will be pursued with the impartial hand of justice,' said the King solemnly; 'in the meantime you will be kept under lock and key in your apartments. Señor Arias, will you kindly accompany us to the Prince's rooms and have them sealed off from the rest of the palace?'

At eleven o'clock that night the Hieronymite monks chanting in the choir of the basilica saw an odd procession pass through their cloisters. It was headed by the King, looking sombre and nervous, followed by the white-faced Queen, Ferdinand, Señores Caballero and Arias, twelve bodyguards bearing torches and a group of masons and locksmiths carrying the tools of their trade.

The sovereigns supervised the imprisonment of their son and then returned to their own apartments to deliberate. The result was a royal manifesto published on the following day which bore the unmistakable stamp of Godoy's romantic prose, and perhaps that of the Queen:

I was living peacefully within the circle of my family when an unknown hand revealed to me the most enormous and unexpected plot which was being formed against my person in my own palace. My successor had planned to dethrone me. I have verified the facts, confronted the Prince, asked the Governor of the Council and other Ministers to begin the prosecution. The guilty parties have been discovered and arrested. My son is confined to his room. I do not wish to conceal from my subjects the profundity of my grief ...

On 31 October Councillor Sebastian de Torres was sent to Toledo to arrest the Canon. He arrived after a forced ride through muddy roads at 7.30 a.m. on 1 November, accompanied by notary Tolero. The Canon gives a vivid account in his memoirs of what ensued:

'Do you have any idea why we have come to arrest you?' Torres asked the Canon.

'I presume it has something to do with my correspondence with the Prince,' the Canon replied, putting a bottle of ink and writing materials into his capacious pockets. Then he asked to be allowed to hear Mass before the little party set off for an unknown destination. The Canon was too upset to be able to eat any breakfast. He was afraid that he was going to be taken to a prison in Asturias or Galicia, perhaps to the castle of San Anton in Corunna where so many political prisoners had languished in their time. Worse still, he might be deported to the Philippines.

The first night was spent in a miserable *posada* and the poor Canon did not sleep a wink. Next day, however, they passed the Puerto de Fuenfria in a biting wind and, recognizing it, the Canon knew that they must be making for Segovia. This raised his hopes, for Segovia is close to the Escorial and so he was more or less assured of having a proper trial.

Later that evening the travellers crossed Segovia and rode up to the Alcazar, the fortress built on a spur above two rivulets at the south-east end of the little town. The mayor of Segovia appeared to be expecting them and while he held a whispered conversation with Torres in one corner the Canon warmed his hands over a brazier at another, next to the mayor's wife who volunteered a few scraps of information about the events of the past two days at the Escorial.

Since there was nothing to eat at the Alcazar Torres took his prisoner to an inn for supper. First he asked the mayor to call a barber as they looked more like brigands than respectable men after their travels. A boy of fourteen was led in; he looked so inexperienced that Torres suggested the Canon be shaved first to see whether or not the lad was capable. The Canon bore the painful operation like a stoic, declaring that the boy was an excellent barber. Torres then confidently placed himself in the boy's hands but – as Escoiquiz observed – his gaoler's moustache was as bristly as a boar's quills and he roared with pain as the rough and ready barber slashed at his hairy face. Escoiquiz could not conceal his glee; fortunately his gaoler had a sense of humour and they both laughed at the joke afterwards.

The next day, as Escoiquiz had anticipated, he was taken to the Escorial and left in a cold, uncomfortable cell without a carpet or a brazier until be began to be interrogated. There he spent eight days without sleeping or eating. By bribing his guards he learned that Ferdinand had made a full confession and that his confederates had been thrown into prison. Finally, in January, he was banished to a monastery near Cordoba where he remained until the following March.

XIX

Meanwhile the Escorial was buzzing with rumours and the hostile reactions to the King's hasty manifesto were causing anxiety to its authors. Although Charles went out hunting unconcernedly every day he was considerably shaken to learn that his people were infuriated by his manifesto and showed signs of contempt and disbelief.

On 30 October, when Charles was at the hunt, Ferdinand asked to be allowed to speak to his mother in private. This was refused but Caballero was sent to his cell to find out what he wanted. It was then, according to Canon Escoiquiz, that the Prince – who must have heard that his father had written to Napoleon – gave him more precise details about his relations with Beauharnais and, through him, Napoleon.

When, upon his return, the King was informed of this confession, both he and the Queen sent for Godoy. What should they do now? This development threw a new light on the drama. What would the Emperor think of all this confusion and dissension? He might begin to reconsider allocating a portion of Portugal to the minister Godoy denounced by implication in Ferdinand's letter of 12 October of which the copy had at last been studied by The

Kings. If Napoleon began to entertain doubts about Godoy's position he might even scrap the treaty and act alone.

In a highly hypocritical and suspect passage of his memoirs, Godoy tries to convince his readers that he was the instrument of a reconciliation between father and son in the interest of all concerned and of the nation at large. He acted as an intermediary, persuaded the Prince to make humble apologies for his conduct and the King to accept them.

Ferdinand was in a state of abject terror, hence his willingness to denounce his friends and make a full confession. He was alone in his room, watched by guards; his own mother checked that the bolts of his apartments were firmly secured at night. It is easy to imagine the fear with which he received the intimation that the Prince of the Peace wished to talk to him. What could he want? What fresh trap was being prepared for him? He could not very well refuse to see the favourite, whom he glared at sullenly when he was ushered in by one of the guards. He hardly raised his head when Godoy saluted him and addressed him unctuously . . . 'kindly', he writes in his memoirs.

'Your Royal Highness,' he began, 'I am grieved to find you in this state and in these circumstances.'

Ferdinand still did not look up.

'I assure you that I am sincere. I intend to be frank with you: Their Majesties have acquainted me with what has happened between you and them. The unknown person who denounced you — yes, I repeat, unknown, for I have not been involved in this unfortunate affair — was not conversant with the facts, which have been exaggerated. In my view, Their Majesties have acted too hastily. They were so horrified by the implications that they jumped to conclusions.'

As Ferdinand looked up, surprised and expectant, Godoy went on:

'I have spoken with the Queen. I have pleaded for her intercession.'

The Prince's eyes filled with tears. Godoy laid a hand on his shoulder.

Prince Ferdinand (later King Ferdinand VII) had a dumpy figure and a crafty character.

Pepita Tudó, the country girl
who became Godoy's mistress,
Countess of Castel-Fiel, and
finally Godoy's second wife.
She deserted him in his
adversity.

San Lorenzo, the monastery-
palace of the Escorial, in which
The Kings imprisoned their
son, Ferdinand, accused of
plotting against their lives.
The Escorial was the bleakest
of all the royal palaces;
Chateaubriand called it 'the
Versailles of the steppes'.

Manuel Godoy, The Kings'
favourite and Queen Maria
Luisa's alleged lover. He was
indolent, sensual and
ambitious.

Princess Maria Antoineta of
Naples, Ferdinand's first,
delicate wife, who died of
consumption.

The *Casita del Labrador* in the gardens of Aranjuez, where the royal family breakfasted in the summer, preferring it to the palace.

Inside the *Casita del Labrador* — the Platinum Hall. This supposedly 'simple' residence was extremely ornate.

'We all make mistakes, Your Royal Highness, and youth is impetuous. You have been ill advised. One must make allowances. That is what I have pointed out to the Queen. I have suggested that the King's manifesto may have been premature.'

'Which manifesto?' Ferdinand knew nothing about it so Godoy filled in the details. At the end of his account the Prince burst into tears.

'Take heart, Ferdinand,' said Godoy gently, 'all is not lost. If you agree to write to your parents begging their forgiveness, the King will take a more lenient view. Furthermore, he will surely have your letters made public.'

Ferdinand darted a suspicious look at Godoy.

'You mean my father wants me to accuse myself in writing? I cannot do that. I shall not. I have done nothing wrong,' he insisted.

'Let me be more explicit,' Godoy went on. 'What I suggest is that you write a short note to your mother to the effect that you repent of the great fault you have committed against her and your father. You wish to beg their pardon and to implore them to forgive the obstinacy of which you were guilty the other evening. You ask the Queen to intercede with the King on your behalf so that he may permit you to kiss his feet. And to the King your father you write that you repent, that you promise him full obedience. You state that you should not have acted without his royal consent, that you were taken off your guard, that you have denounced the guilty parties who advised you and you end by asking for the King's pardon. Now do you see? The blame is in great part removed from your shoulders. You have, I repeat, been ill advised. That is all.'

As Ferdinand was evidently thinking this over, Godoy rose and placed a piece of paper on the chair he had just left. 'Here are the suggested drafts,' he said. 'They are quite simple and straightforward. You have everything to gain by sending these letters to your parents. I suggest you do not delay. The sooner they are made public the better it will be for you.'

On 4 November, while Ferdinand had still not made up his mind whether or not to write the suggested pleas to his parents, The Kings attended a gala reception at the Escorial to celebrate Charles's feast day. Foreign observers noted that they were both very agitated and anxious to bring the festivities to a close.

In his palace off the Prado the fiery Duke of Montijo addressed his assembled retinue as if they had been a private army – which in fact they were:

'His Royal Highness Prince Ferdinand is in danger. No credence can be attached to a manifesto which has so obviously been dictated to His Majesty by the perfidious Godoy. Does anyone – *can* anyone – in his right mind believe that the Prince, who has been brought up according to the strictest principles of duty and religion and who is, as those of us who know him personally can testify, a mild-mannered and peace-loving person, could ever stoop so low as to consider dethroning his father and murdering his mother?'

His remarks were answered by a chorus of gruff cries of: 'Shame! Of course not!' and one realistic peasant voice added: 'How could he, anyway?'

'Exactly,' said the Duke; 'how could he? Such a thought is the product of a disordered and evil imagination; Godoy's. It behoves all of us to protest against the Prince's unlawful imprisonment. The sovereigns must be shown what we Spaniards think about such a vile procedure. I have heard on good authority that it is being planned to take Prince Ferdinand to the prison of Segovia. This must not be allowed. I may be arrested myself at any moment. The Prince's friends and servants are all under suspicion and many of them have already been taken away from Madrid in the middle of the night. Canon Escoiquiz – the Prince's ex-tutor and close adviser – has been thrown into a cell in the Escorial. So far I have been fortunate to escape attention but I fear it will not last. We must therefore act quickly. I want you to help me organize a mass demonstration in favour of His Royal Highness by the peasants of the Guardarrama between the Escorial and Segovia.'

The Duke spread a rough map on the ground and his retinue gathered round it. He pointed to various villages between the two places he had just mentioned.

'Carlos, Enrique, Paco, Antonio, Roberto . . . you will each of you take arms from the cellars and distribute them to the men of these villages. You will divide yourselves into groups and each one will be responsible for leading the peasants to the palace of San Lorenzo to clamour for the Prince's release.'

At dusk on 4 November shouts were heard in the surrounding hills and shots were fired in the air as over one thousand armed peasants under the command of the Duke of Montijo climbed down to the Escorial and marched through the streets in straggly formation proclaiming their allegiance to the Prince and their determination to resist any attempt to have him removed.

The shouts of *'Viva Fernando! Viva el Principe!'* reached the Prince in his cell, and encouraged him to write the letters drafted for him by Godoy. Why not? It was true that he had intrigued behind his parents' back and the Emperor might hold it against him. All things considered, it would be better to have his parents on his side. Above all, he was eager to be released and to see daylight again.

On 5 November his childish little notes were published in the *Madrid Gazette* and subsequently throughout Europe:

Dear Papa: I have been at fault. I have erred to you as King and father but I repent and offer you my most humble expression of obedience. I should not have done anything before giving you notice but I was taken by surprise and have revealed the culprits and I ask you to pardon me. I kiss your feet . . .

Dear Mama: I very much repent of the fault committed against my parents and Kings and with the greatest humility I beg your pardon, also for the obstinacy which led me to keep the truth from you the other night. From the bottom of my heart I entreat you to intercede with Papa so that I may once more be permitted to kiss your feet.

The King wrote:

In view of the above, and at the request of the Queen, my beloved spouse, I pardon my son and will return him to favour as soon as his conduct has given me a proof of his sincere reform.

Justice, however, had to be seen to be believed. A tribunal was appointed under the presidency of Caballero composed of eleven judges, all of them members of the Council of Castile and, as it proved despite all Godoy's efforts, unbribable. The reluctant prosecutor, a partisan of Godoy, Don Simon de Viegas, was so unsure of the outcome that in order to protect himself he wrote a confidential letter which he asked the prior of San Lorenzo to keep under lock and key, to the effect that he had been forced into his role by Godoy.

The King pompously announced: 'The voice of nature disarms all thought of vengeance. My son has denounced the authors of the terrible plot that evil counsellors had suggested to him. All has been declared in due form and in accordance with legal procedure.'

Proceedings against the plotters began on 6 November. (On the insistence of Caballero, Canon Escoiquiz alleges that The Kings were in favour of punishing Ferdinand's accomplices without trial.) On 6 November, too, Ferdinand was allowed to join the royal family's daily outing. A huge crowd gathered on the route. The Kings' carriage met with a stony silence but as soon as Ferdinand appeared he was greeted with enthusiastic cheers.

The court proceeded to Aranjuez, leaving the judges behind in deliberation. The Kings did not dare to pay their customary end of the year visit to Madrid, whose populace was incensed against the whole affair and particularly against Godoy, believed to be at the bottom of it.

On 25 January Caballero and the eleven judges pronounced their verdict: all the accused had been found innocent. One of the judges, Don Eugenio Caballero, had given his verdict on his deathbed, after having received the last sacraments, so eager was he to see that justice was done. His colleagues repaired to his bedroom and each one in turn kissed the crucifix that he grasped in his feeble hands. (In the light of Napoleon's subsequent comments at Bayonne it must be assumed that Beauharnais had been secretly instructed to inform the judges that the Emperor favoured Ferdinand's cause.)

Charles, discomfited by the verdict and no doubt spurred by the vindictive Queen, decided to make use of his royal prerogative. He insisted upon Ferdinand's partisans being banished from the capital. The Duke of Infantado was sent to Ecija in Andalusia and the Canon – as has already been mentioned – to a monastery near Cordoba, where he was treated with the greatest solicitude, as a victim of vengeance.

The question that still puzzled 'the Trinity' was the exact nature of France's role in their son's intrigues. Had the French ambassador acted on his own initiative, or had the Emperor sanctioned the clandestine correspondence? On whose side was he? Charles wrote to Napoleon on 3 November for an explanation of Beauharnais's part in the Escorial affair. The King did not foresee the violence, and duplicity, of the Emperor's reaction.

XX

As soon as Charles's letter reached him, the Emperor summoned Monsieur de Talleyrand (now the Prince of Benevento, from the name of an enclave in the kingdom of Naples).

Monsieur de Talleyrand found the Emperor flushed and excited. He showed Talleyrand the King's letter and exclaimed.

'Well, Monsieur le Prince, and now do you see how right I was about the Bourbons of Spain and their ringleader Godoy?'

What Monsieur de Talleyrand had seen for some time was that Napoleon's ambitions were becoming inordinate; he was alarmed by his master's desire for an ever larger empire. Talleyrand had not signed the secret Treaty of Fontainebleau; he did not agree with the projected partition of Portugal or with Napoleon's increasingly threatening attitude to Spain. He had stated his opinion candidly: 'France ought to remain within her own boundaries; she owes it to her glory, to her sense of justice and of reason, to her own interest and to that of the other nations who will become free. All extensions of territory, all usurpations, by force or by fraud, which have long been connected by prejudice with the idea of rank, of political stability, or superiority in the order of the powers, are only the cruel jests of political lunacy and their real effect is to diminish the happiness and security of the governed for the passing interest or for the vanity of those who govern.'

These were not the words that the Emperor wanted to hear.

'Do you not see,' he insisted, 'how impossible it is to have dealings with such corrupt, intriguing individuals who, moreover, are totally devoid of dignity? I have spoken to Azara, the Spanish ambassador . . . ' (Spoken? The Emperor had bellowed. His voice had been heard all over the palace of Fontainebleau.)

'I told him bluntly that when I received the King of Spain's letter of 29 October I did not make any comments at the time because the matter was none of my business and I had no desire to be involved in a family dispute. But now, since this further letter has arrived, I have every reason to be profoundly irritated. I have asked the Spanish ambassador to send a courier to Madrid to inform the court that I never received any letter from the Prince of Asturias and that I shall not countenance any intrigues. From now on I shall take the Prince under my wing. If anybody dares to touch or insult him, and if the combined Franco-Spanish army does not leave immediately for Portugal in accordance with our recently signed convention, I shall declare war on Spain. I shall place myself at the head of my army to invade her . . . I shall recall my ambassador and dismiss the Spanish ambassador from Paris. That is what I told Azara. Furthermore, I will not have Beauharnais's name brought up in the judicial proceedings taking place in Spain. I have made that perfectly clear.'

'I trust that your discourse impressed the Spanish ambassador?' hazarded Monsieur de Talleyrand.

Napoleon looked at him sharply. Monsieur de Talleyrand was smiling. He had known his master too long not to know when he was feigning a lion-like anger.

'Monsieur de Azara was pulverized,' Napoleon replied cheerfully. 'He was shaking so violently when he left me that I thought he would fall before he reached the door. Now I shall follow up our conversation [monologue would have been a more accurate word] by writing a personal letter to King Charles. Monsieur le Prince, I wish you to summon Godoy's agent, Señor Izquierdo, to Fontainebleau. Tell him, in the strongest possible terms, how very angry I am. I insist that the treaty be carried out and I refuse to be implicated, personally or through my ambassador in Madrid, in this sordid affair of the Escorial. I absolutely forbid any mention of our names in the proceedings. Izquierdo will of course defend Godoy and pretend that he has had nothing to do with it but I know better. That man is a menace to everybody. He has tricked me systematically since 1801 and that comic-opera War of the Oranges.'

'With the aid of your brother Lucien,' Talleyrand interjected.

'You do not have to remind me,' said Napoleon curtly. 'Lucien continues to thwart me. He now refuses to allow me to offer his daughter Charlotte in marriage to the Prince of Asturias. There is no other candidate available so that possibility will have to be abandoned. It is unimportant, anyway. By all accounts the Prince is mediocre, easily swayed – he will be dealt with when the time comes.'

What was brewing in the Emperor's mind? Did he really plan to invade Spain? Was there a grain of truth in what he had said to the Spanish ambassador? Perhaps it would be wise to slip a few veiled insinuations to Izquierdo so that he could warn the court of Spain through Godoy. That was what passed through Monsieur de Talleyrand's mind as he listened to his master, from whom he was gradually detaching himself. He had no wish to be dragged down with him, a process which he perceived was about to begin.

In his view, there was no difficulty or disagreement, national or international, that could not be solved through negotiations — preferably held in private round a well provided dinner table. It was said that he paid his chef the same salary as an ambassador. He was, in fact, convinced that a good chef was capable of achieving the same results as a diplomat. The Emperor, who gobbled his meals in ten minutes, would never agree to such a civilized way of conducting affairs. Where would all his military campaigns lead to? Monsieur de Talleyrand left him, full of gloomy forebodings.

XXI

On 18 November Izquierdo received stern instructions from Napoleon, transmitted by Monsieur de Champagny, the Minister for External Affairs, formally demanding that no allusion was to be made in the Escorial deliberations either to him or to his ambassador. There was to be no inkling that the French had intervened in Spain's internal affairs.

But the question of a French wife for Ferdinand was mooted, and Charles himself asked the Emperor whether this would not be possible. Mademoiselle Tascher de la Pagerie had been married in the meantime and Lucien's daughter Charlotte was the only unmarried Princess available. But, as we have seen, Lucien refused to part with her. The Emperor therefore prudently ignored Charles's reference to a French marriage. Godoy, on his side, took up the matter and began corresponding with the financier Michel for the hand of Murat's neice. He wished to prove that he had the Prince's interests at heart, since the scales appeared to be tilting in the heir's favour.

After the verdict of the Escorial tribunal had been made public and Napoleon had received a detailed report of the proceedings, he asked Champagny to have a pamphlet written and translated into Spanish. Although the order for its publication was ultimately cancelled, the text dictated by the Emperor throws an interesting light upon his opinion of the Spanish court at the time; furthermore, it proves that he believed in the tittle-tattle on the subject of the Queen's amorous relations and amours which had been recounted to him years before by Monsieur Alquier:

'Ferdinand must be declared to be innocent of the Escorial plot,' he told Champagny, 'but he must be described as unfit to ascend the throne. You must paint the Queen and King as they are: he is a good man, but lacking in character or culture. Stress the riches and extortions of Godoy, give details of his criminal affair with the Queen, his role as procuror with regard to guardsman Mallo and others (put with delicacy but none the less effectively). Dwell on Godoy's corruption and the decadence of the kingdom, also on the shameful fact that Spain is not mistress of Gibraltar.'

This scurrilous manifesto was shelved, probably because Napoleon was hesitating between two variations on the Spanish theme: the first was his desire to secure the northern provinces of Spain above the Ebro, the second was the means whereby he could dethrone the Spanish Bourbons.

The great 19th-century novelist Perez Galdós summed up the Spanish people's verdict on the Escorial affair as follows. He puts the words into the mouth of a simple man of the people.

I'm sure the Prince isn't worth much, but this can only be said between ourselves. When the Princess of Asturias was alive everybody said that Ferdinand was the enemy of the French and of Napoleon because they helped Godoy, and now it seems the French people are the best in the world and Napoleon is as good as blessed bread only because he's helped Ferdinand's cause. This isn't right, and as I see it, the heir wishes to succeed long before his father dies. The Canon of Toledo and others have him under their thumb and would be capable of turning him into a bad son so long as they are sure of obtaining good positions at court. These high-ups are ambitious folk. They talk a lot about the well-being of the state when all they really want is power to order people about. Although they haven't taught us how to read or write, I am pretty shrewd and I have a good idea of who's who and what's going on; we may appear to be nitwits but we sometimes guess the truth more accurately than the know-alls and can predict what's going to happen. That's why you must believe me when I tell you that we are going to go through rough times — mark my words — very rough times.

Distrust was increasing on both sides of the frontier. Napoleon was not only irritated by the Spanish contretemps, which caused him to speculate about the future of his relations with Spain; he was also highly dissatisfied with the turn of events in Portugal. He had heard from his brother Joseph in Naples on 4 November that General John Moore, with 7,000 men, had left Sicily for an unknown destination believed to be Portugal.

The terrified Regent held a Council of State during the night of 9/10 November when it was decided that if Franco-Spanish troops passed the frontier the entire Portuguese court would embark for Brazil with the royal treasury, archives and chief ministers.

Portugal had signed a secret convention with England on 22 October. Foreign Secretary Canning promised to send six ships and 5,000 men to cover the embarkation of the Regent for Brazil in exchange for concessions to British trade in that country, and Sidney Smith was ordered to secure the Portuguese squadron by negotiations or by force. Lord Strangford joined Smith's squadron as it approached Lisbon, in a fishing boat, and strongly advised him not to use force; the Portuguese coastal batteries were ready for action and there were several Russian ships outside the harbour (Russia had declared war against England in October 1807).

The Treaty of Fontainebleau had provided that if the

English sent an army to Portugal the Emperor would reinforce Junot's corps after giving due notice to the King of Spain. With this excuse a corps of 25,000 men under General Dupont had been assembled at Bayonne. On 22 November Dupont received orders to cross the Bidassoa, although no English force had been heard of. No intimation of this movement was sent to the court of Spain and both Charles and Godoy were shaken and astonished when they heard that French troops were pouring down the valley of the Ebro.

The Portuguese Regent delayed his departure until the last minute. If he had hesitated two hours longer he would not have been able to leave at all because of a terrible storm that blew up through the night.

The next day, 30 November, posters appeared all over Lisbon announcing the impending arrival of Junot who entered the capitol at the head of his bedraggled troops on 1 December in the middle of a rainstorm. Most of his soldiers were in rags and shoeless. Nevertheless, he sent off a cheerful report to Napoleon to tell him that they had met with an enthusiastic reception.

In a cool reply from Milan, Napoleon wrote:

You are like men who have no experience of conquests; you delude yourself with such illusions. The situation is disquieting; misery, famine, English spies and intrigues all over the country; the ghost of the Prince Regent haunting the coast. And the people are your enemies. I do not recognize in you a man brought up in my school. You are in a vanquished country and you behave as if you were in Burgundy.

He ordered Junot to confiscate English goods in Lisbon and arrest British citizens who were to be sent to France.

On 20 December Napoleon sent word to Junot that his army 'must be in a position to make a detour and march elsewhere either in whole or in part'. The occupation of the entire Spanish peninsula was beginning to grip the Emperor's mind.

Junot had now become less optimistic; he complained that the Spaniards were not keeping to their side of the Fontainebleau bargain. They were supposed to supply the

French army with Galician beef and Castilian wheat but none
was forthcoming. His men were half-famished. Not for the
first time, the Spanish were dragging their feet. Napoleon was
exasperated and he began to show an iron hand. Had he not
waited long enough? Only a show of force would bring the
reluctant Spaniards to heel. Was he already looking farther
ahead? It is very likely. He had more than once expressed his
poor opinion of the Spanish Bourbons; recent events – the
Escorial family dispute – had confirmed his views. As for
Godoy, he had a string of grievances against the favourite: his
double-deal at the time of the War of the Oranges, his
backing out of the subsidies' treaty after 1803, his failure to
supply sufficient ships to France on time, now his failure to
send provisions to French troops as had been agreed at
Fontainebleau. At the end of January 1808 *Le Moniteur*
– which Napoleon often used to air schemes which were on
the point of being implemented – abused Godoy as a bad
minister for Spain and a false friend to France.

On 1 February Junot published a decree from Lisbon to the
effect that from henceforth the kingdom of Portugal would
be administered by him alone. This was a flagrant contra-
vention of the partition agreed upon at Fontainebleau.
Godoy retorted by bringing back the Spanish troops from the
Algarve and the Alentejo – the southern provinces of Portugal which he had hoped would constitute his own private
little kingdom. Troops were also recalled from Andalusia
where they had been dispatched to prevent a threatened
landing by General Moore and his men.

In the north a French army corps under Marshal Moncey
occupied Biscay and Navarre. Dupont pushed forward to
Burgos and Valladolid. A Franco-Italian division of 14,000
men under General Duchesne began to pour into Catalonia.
Catalonia is not on the way to Portugal, and there was no
excuse for the entrance of a French army in the north-east.
Barcelona was taken by ruse. General Duchesne ordered a
review of his troops; after a few manoeuvres they appeared to

withdraw to the south of the city but suddenly they made a volte-face, marched back past the gates of the citadel, wheeled left and made an unexpected attack upon the fortress, whose rightful occupants were ousted by nightfall.

A similar stratagem was used in Pamplona, Navarre, where the French troops were quartered in the lower part of the town. Snow began to fall; a large party of French soldiers gathered outside the fortress gates and engaged in a sham snowball fight. At a given signal the losing side rushed up to the gates pursued by their comrades; they knocked down the unsuspecting sentries, and seized the muskets stacked in the guards' room. They were soon reinforced by a company of grenadiers followed by a battalion which had been drilling a few yards away from the fortress.

The Spanish court was at long last seriously alarmed. Charles sent an anxious letter to Napoleon on 5 February recalling his past services and asking for an explanation of the present situation which, he confessed, he found 'not at all reassuring'.

Godoy wrote despondently to Izquierdo on 9 February:

I live in a state of uncertainty. The treaty you concluded does not exist any more. The kingdom is full of troops. We have been asked for what remains of our squadrons. All is uncertainty, intrigue, fear for the future. The allied troops live at our expense. In Paris you are not in good odour. What does all this mean? And where will it all end?

Napoleon's curt reply to Charles's letter of 5 February was devious and uncivil. He remarked that the King had not mentioned Ferdinand's marriage and asked what his intentions were; he was simply playing for time. 'I want to place all my brothers upon thrones,' he had once declared. Did he broach the subject of the Spanish throne with Joseph when they met in Italy in February 1808, and did Joseph's reluctance to accept it (at that time) cause the Emperor to delay and change his tactics? It is possible, but there is no documentary evidence to prove it one way or the other.

PART FIVE

THE ARANJUEZ UPRISING
AND THE KINGS' ABDICATION

XXII

Meanwhile, a person who had recently seen the Emperor arrived on 19 February at Aranjuez: Luisetta, the dispossessed Queen of Etruria, with her little son Charles and sixty carriages of effects, one of which contained the embalmed corpse of her late husband Louis which she wished to deposit in the vaults of San Lorenzo.

The Princess's belongings were nothing, she told her parents, compared to what she had had to leave behind her in Florence. She had had to give away some of her best horses. 'General Aubusson, who came to preside over my departure at the Pitti palace, actually forbade me to remove several pieces of furniture which were very dear to me. He could not wait to take over lock, stock and barrel. The people of Florence too behaved abominably.' They ran to the Princess from all sides calling for arrears of salaries and for gratifications. They insulted her when she refused, for lack of money. What was this new kingdom that had been promised to her for her son: she had only heard about it when she reached Milan . . . Why had the negotiations been hidden from her?

The Kings tried to pacify her and explain that the treaty of Fontainebleau was a secret one and that they had not been able to forewarn their daughter of the clause about Etruria. On the other hand they were not very reassuring. How had Napoleon behaved towards Luisetta, they wanted to know? How had he appeared to her? 'Very rude,' she said. He had told her that she could wait in Nice if she liked until her new kingdom was ready, and he said that the suggestion of a kingdom in Portugal had come from her own parents.

The day after Luisetta's arrival at Aranjuez Godoy learned that Napoleon's brother-in-law Murat (recently appointed Grand Duke of Berg and Cleves from a tiny Rhineland duchy given to him by the Emperor) had been appointed the

Emperor's lieutenant commander in Spain. It was well known that the former innkeeper's son and handsome hussar, the most daring horseman in Europe, full of elan and Gascon braggadocio, was a specialist of the sudden, spectacular coup. His nomination did not inspire confidence at court.

Only Luisetta spoke up in his favour. 'The Grand Duke of Berg is a charming man,' she exclaimed when Godoy brought the news of his appointment to the palace. Murat was a favourite with the ladies; he had panache, he was a good mixer, he was elegant. An envious colleague observed caustically: 'Murat is all curls and finery; his clothes would grace the wardrobe of a strolling player.'

Godoy, who had exchanged presents and a warm correspondence with Murat, was dubious. In the new circumstances that were developing daily Murat could prove dangerous. What lay behind his appointment? At that precise moment it is possible that the Emperor himself was not sure.

'It would be dangerous to frighten the Spaniards,' he told Murat, and on 14 March he ordered him to reassure The Kings and Godoy because 'I want to remain friends with Spain and fulfil my political objective without resorting to hostilities. I hope that everything can be settled satisfactorily.'

To this effect Napoleon had sent a list of fresh propositions to Madrid, transmitted verbally to Izquierdo by Duroc and Talleyrand, to be confided to the King alone. Izquierdo arrived at Aranjuez on 5 March. The recent French moves, Izquierdo had been asked to explain to The Kings, were aimed at disarming the English party in Spain. England had spread the rumour that the Emperor was favourable to Prince Ferdinand so as to bring about a break with France and, by helping Spain, England would have a territory from which to set fire to the entire continent. To prevent English influence and put a stop to the internal struggles of the Spanish factions, France had begun to invade the Kingdom and had occupied frontier posts 'by pacific and innocent methods' since these posts had not been opened spontaneously as the

treaty of Fontainebleau obliged them to ... English contra-
band along the Spanish coasts was still rife and the Spaniards
appeared to be doing little to stop it. The Spanish squadron
had not yet joined the French fleet at Toulon to relieve the
blockade of Cadiz.

His Majesty's loyalty was not in doubt but his minister's
was. The Emperor had heard that an anarchist party had been
formed who were anxious to establish a constitution of an
English or American type (this was a contradiction in terms)
in Spain. Since a revolution would prevent freedom of action,
His Majesty was urged to adhere to his agreements with
France. The French troops, said the Emperor, were in a
difficult position. They were liable to be attacked both by
the English and by the Spaniards. Because of the changed
interior policy of Spain since the signing of the Treaty of
Fontainebleau, the Emperor no longer considered himself
bound to fulfil its clauses. He foresaw a civil war in Spain so
he intended to occupy peacefully the frontier provinces with
France. These, he suggested, could be exchanged for Portugal. The Emperor had returned to his idea of annexing all of
Spain north of the Ebro.

He also broached the subject of Ferdinand: 'If the Prince
had not been completely pardoned, the throne would have
passed to another of Charles's sons [as the King had himself
declared at the time of the Escorial affair]. The Emperor
wished to be fully acquainted with the facts before going into
the question of a family alliance. Thirdly, he suggested a
commercial treaty, a revival of the old 'Family Pact' between
France and Spain. He had asked Izquierdo, too, whether
there was any truth in a rumour that had reached Paris to the
effect that The Kings were planning to remove themselves to
Andalusia.

Charles convened a ministerial conference at Aranjuez
which Ferdinand was allowed to attend. Godoy described the
conference in his memoirs.

'Now that we have recalled our troops from Portugal and
the south,' Godoy told the meeting, 'we could perhaps make

a show of resistance.'

'Show indeed,' repeated Don Pedro Cevallos, the Secretary of State, 'for we have neither the arms nor the organized forces necessary to oppose any serious resistance to the French and they know it. Napoleon has planted spies everywhere. Madrid is riddled with them and his so-called "observers" .'

'I do not want any bloodshed,' said Charles firmly. 'It would be a blot on my reign and would not serve any useful purpose.'

'Then, Your Majesties, gentlemen, if you are all agreed that armed resistance is useless, there is only one other course open, and that is for the court to follow the example of that of Portugal and take refuge in South America – perhaps Peru?' suggested Godoy.

'It is too far,' the King objected. 'I could not endure such a long voyage.'

'I agree with His Majesty,' interjected the Queen. 'Why could we not go to Andalusia where we still have troops to protect us? Seville, for instance. Then, if things get worse, we would be near the port of Cadiz if we finally decided to set sail.'

'I am of the opinion that we should stay here and not desert our posts,' said the King. 'Are we going to allow the French to walk into Madrid and take over without a murmur of dissent? If we run away it will give them an opportunity to replace us.'

'Well said, sire,' said Ferdinand. All turned towards the Prince, surprised to hear his voice raised at a conference. The Prince reddened but went on: 'I for one will not leave for the south. We must make a firm stand here.'

'I shan't leave either,' piped Don Antonio, the King's brother.

'This is no time for Quixotic decisions,' objected Godoy. 'What kind of a "stand" can we make? Cevallos is right. We must be realistic.'

The deliberations went on for hours, were interrupted for

supper, then resumed on the following days, with dissensions between the various members of the royal family and the ministers. With every day that passed the news was more disquieting: a fifth French army corps under Bessières had now begun to cross the Bidassoa. There were over 100,000 French soldiers south of the Pyrenees.

Godoy advised instant flight without any attempt to defend Madrid or central Spain.

Cases of bullion were secretly transported to the palace from the capital; servants were seen moving chests and trunks along the palace corridors and through the courtyards, checking and polishing the royal carriages and harnesses. It was obvious that the royal departure was imminent.

On 10 March Izquierdo left Aranjuez and had a talk with Godoy in Madrid before returning to Paris with The Kings' counter-proposals. They considered that the cession of Portugal south of the Ebro was an insufficient compensation for the Spanish territory to the north, and suggested that a new kingdom should be constituted from the provinces on the left bank of the Ebro which would be called the 'Vice-Royalty of Iberia', respecting the laws and privileges of the inhabitants, with the heir of Etruria at its head. This solution had been advanced by Luisetta. Charles, on his side, wished to retain his title of 'Emperor of the Americas' – a hollow crown indeed! By the time Izquierdo got back to Paris events had superseded the King's reply to the Emperor.

Murat was on his way to Vitoria amid the hurrahs and cries of 'Viva Napoleon' of the ignorant populace. He wrote to the Emperor on the 14th that he had heard Godoy was mobilizing troops against the people of Madrid who were on the point of revolting, and that he – Godoy – had sent his personal effects to a northern port. Furthermore, Godoy had ordered the mobilization of the southern Spanish Troops. 'If there is any opposition,' he assured Napoleon on the 15th, 'I shall send my troops out en masse to fight against the Spaniards.'

Napoleon had dispatched the Count of Tournon-Simiane to Madrid in the role of observer. He was one of several independent experts sent to Spain by the Emperor during the first months of 1808; the most level-headed and the most perceptive. The Count reported that he had had a ten minute interview with Godoy on 12 March; he had spoken to him about the French troops and

he appeared to be very occupied . . . His police is well organized. He has 10,000 or 12,000 men posted round Madrid. Everyone hates him. This man must be sacrificed; it is the only way in which the taking of Pamplona and Barcelona would be mitigated. Fortunately, Godoy is supposed to be the author of all the evils that beset Spain.

Tournon sent a further dispatch twenty-four hours later. 'A person of confidence' had informed him that the court was preparing to leave for Andalusia, somewhere near Gibraltar

although the King refuses to at the moment, but the Queen and Godoy hope to convince him. If the court and troops move down there it will be difficult to get anything out of them by force because at the first setback they will have recourse to the open sea and America. Spain without its colonies would be a burden. The Spanish colonials are much more active· than the Spaniards and in a few years will be able to dispense with Europe and establish their own manufactures. The emigration of the court would consolidate the colonies. Would it be expedient to make Godoy an offer? His present precarious position might make him amenable.

XXIII

At the palace of Aranjuez, Ferdinand and a group of his friends, including the Dukes of Hijar, Montijo, the Count of Frias and the Count of Fernan Nuñez, as well as his uncle Don Antonio, held a hastily convened meeting which Canon Escoiquiz related in his memoirs, although he was not present. (Ferdinand recalled him from his exile near Cordoba on 16 March.)

'Godoy is pressing Their Majesties to leave for Andalusia,' the Prince informed his coterie, 'and he has already dispatched several cases of his valuables to the Ferrol for safety. This departure, gentlemen, must be prevented at all costs. The people must be alerted. I have been told that Godoy intends to ask for troops from the Madrid garrison to cover the intended flight. What do you propose we should do?'

'In my opinion,' said the Duke of Montijo, ever ready for a coup, 'all of us present should instruct our guards and manservants to spread the news among the populace and encourage them to follow the soldiers from Madrid to Aranjuez. We shall then have a friendly-disposed crowd available to surround Godoy's palace and prevent him from leaving it. That is a first step . . . '

'It is indeed essential to separate Godoy from Their Majesties,' agreed the Duke of Hijar. 'Without him the plan is bound to fail.'

'But we shall have to do more than that,' said the Prince. 'We shall have to confine Godoy to his residence, or – '

'Or make him prisoner?' suggested the Duke of Montijo. 'Let us leave the crowds to do this of their own accord. We do not want to be held responsible for what may happen later.'

'We shall nevertheless have to lead the crowd,' said the Duke of Hijar. 'We must, however discreetly, give the initial impetus.'

'I am quite willing to do so,' cried the Duke of Montijo. 'I can disguise myself as a peasant and move from group to group fomenting the excitement.'

'Not too much excitement,' Ferdinand cautioned. 'We do not want Godoy to be torn limb from limb and to start a bloody revolution. He must be properly tried – as I was.'

'The populace must demand Godoy's resignation – the cry must come from them,' declared the Count of Frias.

'They will not have to be goaded to do that,' said the Duke of Hijar. 'And then, gentlemen, what next?'

The Duke of Montijo was the first to voice the thought that must have crossed the mind of all those present. 'If Godoy is made to resign, Their Majesties will be at a complete loss. It will not require much pressure to persuade His Majesty to abdicate.'

'And then . . .' All eyes turned to the Prince.

'Let us not anticipate, gentlemen; there is still much to be done and life is unpredictable,' he replied.

The Duke of Hijar expressed qualms. 'None of us have referred to the French or to the Emperor, who may have his own private plans for us. I find it strange that he has not replied to His Royal Highness's letter of 12 October about the proposed marriage with a French princess and to his appeal for protection.'

'It is not strange,' objected the Count of Frias. 'It is perfectly natural. The Emperor is being discreet. We are all of us aware that he intervened in His Royal Highness's favour during the Escorial affair. Beauharnais would not have lied to us about that. He did not wish their names to be mentioned, but nevertheless they were all for us. Now it is up to us to give the Emperor the opportunity to assist us further. He cannot be expected to have double dealings: with Their Majesties and Godoy on the one hand and with the Prince on the other. See how he is treating Godoy! He is playing him like a salmon. He holds him in utter contempt. Once Godoy is removed, and that is for us to accomplish, and after our further main objective has been achieved — the Emperor's way will be clear and we shall soon arrive at an understanding with him.'

So, at the very moment that Godoy was trying to persuade The Kings to make a determined stand and escape from French clutches, Ferdinand and his party prepared to trust the Emperor and play into his hands.

On 14 March, when Godoy arrived at Aranjuez from Madrid, he found The Kings greatly agitated by another anonymous note which had been left on the King's table in the same mysterious manner as the Escorial warning. This one, however, was in a different handwriting:

An awful fate lies in store for Your Majesty if the court leaves Aranjuez — Izquierdo is a traitor and should be arrested . . .

Godoy advised The Kings to talk the matter over with Ferdinand whom he guessed to be the author of the note. During their confrontation the King suggested that if Ferdinand did not wish to leave for Seville he could remain behind as his lieutenant with a court of his own; he stipulated, however (according to Godoy's memoirs), that Canon Escoiquiz should be excluded from the Prince's entourage. The Kings would justify their journey south on the grounds of health. Ferdinand appeared to be in an acquiescent mood and was even affectionate to Godoy, whom he embraced; but on 15 March his partisans advised against the plan, even though Beauharnais had just transmitted an imperial order to Godoy asking for permission to allow 50,000 French troops to cross Madrid en route for Cadiz, on the slim pretext that the city was menaced by English naval forces.

It was not necessary for the Duke of Montijo's lackeys to inform the people of Madrid about what was happening at Aranjuez. They had heard about the King's preparations to leave the palace and were unanimous in their desire to oppose it, ready in their Quixotic Spanish way to face the enemy with their bare fists and defend The Kings and Ferdinand to their last gasp. Groups of men and women travelled unceasingly between the capital and Aranjuez in carts or on foot; peasants, tradesmen, farm labourers gathered before the palace to voice their anxiety.

Charles was forced to issue a proclamation which was posted at the palace gates, assuring his people that he had no intention of leaving his good city of Madrid, nor his palace of Aranjuez, and that he would stay with his faithful subjects. He made a personal appearance on the balcony and was loudly cheered. But a few dissident voices rose from the assembled crowd: 'Down with Godoy! The French are invading Spain — Godoy has let them in!'

As the mob continued to agitate in front of the palace, he issued a second proclamation:

Your noble agitation in the circumstances is a further proof of your sentiments and I who love you as tenderly as a father hasten to console you in your present state of anguish. Be calm. The army of my dear ally is crossing the kingdom in peace and friendship. His object is to move his troops to those points where there is a danger of an enemy disembarkation, and the assembly of the corps of my guards neither has the object to defend me nor to accompany me in a journey which malicious tongues have induced you to believe is imminent.

This announcement was received with demonstrations of joy and shouts of *'Viva el Rey'*. But as troops continued to arrive from Madrid the mob became restive again and there were more cries of 'Down with Godoy! Down with the traitor!'

XXIV

At 6.30 a.m. on 17 March Don Carlos Velasco, an officer from the general staff of the Madrid garrison, rode up to Government House in the Puerta del Sol and asked for an urgent interview with the Governor.

That gentleman cursed roundly as he hurriedly put on his dressing-gown and slippers and stumbled, bleary-eyed, into the ante-room where Don Carlos was waiting for him.

'What brings you here at such an unearthly hour?' he grumbled.

'I apologize, sir, but the matter is both urgent and grave. I would like to have your advice. An hour ago I received verbal instructions from a courier dispatched at full gallop from the Prince of the Peace at Aranjuez. I was promised that written instructions would follow within the half hour but they have not come. I have been asked to send to the palace of Aranjuez, at once, the Walloon guards, the carabiniers and other corps of the Madrid garrison. I thought that you and the council should be informed of such an unprecedented request.'

The Governor was perplexed. 'You are right, Don Carlos, this is a very irregular procedure. No written instructions? Nothing from His Majesty? It sounds as though the royal family are about to leave Aranjuez and require military protection. I entreat you, do nothing. Nothing, until I have convened an extraordinary meeting of the council, by which time you may have received a written order. Even so, in the present uncertain circumstances I doubt whether we should act on the sole command of the Prince of the Peace. Let us therefore wait and keep in touch with one another. Thank you, Don Carlos, for informing me so soon. I shall keep you au fait with our deliberations.'

Don Carlos was far from anxious to comply with the orders from Aranjuez, particularly since they came from a man whom everybody felt – and hoped – was at last about to be toppled. The people were working themselves up to boiling point and were being encouraged by the Prince's partisans. Did Godoy intend to provoke a *coup de main*? Had he persuaded The Kings to make a furtive escape with the Prince under cover of the military? The longer the dispatch of troops to Aranjuez was delayed the better the chance of warning the Prince and getting him away from the palace. With these thoughts in his mind, Don Carlos returned to barracks to await further developments.

The members of the council were equally disturbed; they too decided to adopt delaying tactics. A courier, however, reached the Governor by mid-morning with a request, signed by Charles, to make a public announcement that the King, the faithful ally of the French Emperor, had asked for troops as a precautionary measure so as not to 'risk being insulted by isolated partisans in an unfortified residence'. Godoy must have got wind of the Prince's plan.

The council agreed not to publish the announcement until they had sent and received a reply to a strongly-worded protest to the King, pointing out that the effect of sending troops to Aranjuez might provoke an armed rebellion which would endanger the royal family. The council sat in permanent session all day in the midst of a stream of contradictory reports and rumours.

At nightfall Don Carlos Velasco sent word to the Governor that he had at last received written instructions from Godoy in his capacity of Generalissimo and was therefore obliged to obey his orders and leave for Aranjuez with his troops. The Governor and civil authorities had no power to prevent their departure.

The crowds which the soldiers crossed on the road to Aranjuez were a mixture of people of all classes: honest citizens, picaresque rogues, ardent royalist fanatics, curious idlers with no political leanings. Most of them did not know exactly why they were going to Aranjuez or what they would do once they reached their destination; they merely sensed (with a primitive's intuition) that there was danger in the air and an opportunity for action.

In Aranjuez itself the mood of the crowd was distinctly belligerent for they had seen the bustle round the palace which presaged a flight. When the troops arrived from Madrid and encircled the palace, forcing the crowds back towards the town centre, they were greeted by anxious cries: 'Don't allow The Kings to leave us! Don't let them go! The Prince appeared at a window and told us that The Kings were about to depart . . . don't let Godoy escape.'

Godoy hurried back to his residence from the royal palace by one of the back doors soon after dark. His wife and Pepita Tudó were busy packing. He ordered a coach to be driven up to the front gate at half past eleven with an escort of personal bodyguards to take Pepita Tudó to Madrid with instructions to supervise the transfer of his valuables from his two palaces in the capital.

A man in labourer's clothes yet with a noble bearing, who called himself 'Tio Pedro' and invited people freely for drinks in the taverns of Aranjuez, distributed posters inscribed:

'Long live the King! Long live the Prince of Asturias! Death
to that dog Godoy!' He was the adventure-loving Duke of
Montijo in disguise, rousing the populace as he had done
before at the Escorial. (For an account of the events at
Aranjuez the present author has used that of an objective
eye-witness, Brissy, an equerry attached to Ferdinand, whose
manuscript has been preserved in the royal archives of
Madrid.)

Little by little, 'Tio Pedro' led the masses towards Godoy's
house. When the coach drove up, the front door opened
quickly disclosing the figure of a heavily draped woman who
ran between two rows of guards and climbed into the waiting
carriage; the coachman whipped up the horses and shouted:
'Make way or you will all be trampled to death!' The
frightened horses reared, the coachman cursed and the
woman inside – some said it was Pepita Tudó – screamed
with fear. The crowds pressed against the bodyguard; there
was a scuffle, angry voices were raised in protest, a shot was
fired and a bugle sounded in the distance. At this signal 'Tio
Pedro' pushed his way forward yelling at the top of his voice:
'Come on citizens, do not be afraid. Down with the traitor!
What are we waiting for? What have we come for? Justice –
let us find Godoy!'

'Let us find Godoy!' shrieked the rabble, surging forward
and overpowering the bodyguards. In no time they forced the
doors and swept through the house like locusts, overturning
the furniture and smashing the precious china in the cabinets.
In the sitting-room a terrified woman was clutching a child to
her skirts; she was immediately recognized as the Countess of
Chinchón, Godoy's wife, and courteously escorted to the
royal palace. Everybody was aware that she had been forced
to marry Godoy and that she hated him as much as they did.
She was reported to have said that she hated her child
because it reminded her of its father.

The mob rushed upstairs and into the bedrooms, their rage
mounting as they saw that their quarry had eluded them. Was
it possible that they had been duped, that the draped figure

in the coach had been Godoy in disguise? Perhaps he had
gone to the royal palace. 'To the palace! To the palace!'
shouted one of the self-appointed leaders, and back they
poured in reverse.

But Godoy was still in his house. Panting with fear, he had
raced up to the attics as soon as he had heard the screeching
mob and hidden himself inside a dusty roll of old carpets
where he spent an agonizing night.

XXV

Inside the royal palace the sovereigns and their entourage
took refuge in the drawing-room overlooking the gardens
where the crowds had taken up their position before the
arrival of the troops. They too were trembling with fear.
Only Ferdinand remained grave and calm. In the space of a
few hours he had acquired a poise and maturity which filled
his parents with foreboding.

'What is happening? Who has incited the people to
surround the palace?' Charles asked querulously. 'The troops
came so late yet I know that Manuel sent for them at dawn.
Why didn't they come before?'

'We cannot leave now,' said Luisetta. 'We are prisoners in
our own palace. That does not, however, appear to trouble
you, Ferdinand!'

The Prince crossed over to one of the windows and peered
through the curtains.

'Do something, Ferdinand!' the Queen implored her son as
the shouts of 'Down with Godoy!' grew louder and more
insistent. 'Can't you quieten the crowd? I am afraid they will
force their way into the palace.'

'It is too dark, mother. They will not be able to see my
face and I cannot show a light,' the Prince answered.

'Why not?' cried the Queen suspiciously. 'Why can't you
show a light? Is that a pre-arranged signal, then? What devilry
are you up to now?'

At that moment the bugle call sounded. Ferdinand seized a lamp from a nearby table and stepped briskly on to the balcony. The crowds raised a joyful shout. So the Prince was safe – he had not left! From the distance came the sounds of shots and the yelling of the mob as they hurled themselves against the doors of Godoy's residence.

Maria Luisa started up. 'They have gone to Manuel's house!' she gasped. 'Ferdinand, Ferdinand, you *must* help – you *must* put a stop to this massacre!'

'Yes, this must be stopped,' said the King firmly, rising and hobbling across the room on his gouty feet to confront his son.

'I cannot stop it, sire,' said Ferdinand. 'Nobody can. You are listening to the pent-up fury of a people who are at the end of their tether. They will no longer endure the corrupt tyranny of Godoy. I tried to warn you, sire, but you refused to believe me. You punished and imprisoned me for my pains. You would not listen to your son – listen now to the voice of Spain!' He opened the windows wide and the angry cries of the mob echoed through the room.

'Shut the windows, shut the windows!' the King beseeched him.

'The voice of Spain!' the Queen repeated sarcastically. 'They are a pack of wild animals. Manuel is in danger. I must send someone to find out what has become of him.' She rang for a footman to be dispatched to the favourite's residence. 'Tell him to find out what has happened and to report back to me as soon as possible,' she demanded.

Half an hour later the footman returned and said that nobody knew where Godoy was. The crowds had surged back and were clamouring fiercely for the favourite, believing that he had taken refuge within the palace.

Don Pedro Cevallos and Caballero asked for an audience. They took a grave view of the situation and advised the King to take action.

'What action?' asked the King petulantly.

Ferdinand walked over to the ministers. 'Gentlemen,' he began, and the new note of authority in his voice surprised them all, 'Gentlemen, I believe I can guess what is in your minds and what you hesitate to say to my revered parents. Correct me if I am wrong. Public hostility against the Prince of the Peace has reached such a pitch that he will indubitably lose his life, unless – unless he is dismissed from his posts of Generalissimo and Admiral of the Fleet.'

'Dismissed? You want us to dismiss Manuel?' The Queen was horrified. 'Is that really what you think, gentlemen, or is this another sinister plot?'

'This is no plot, Madam,' Don Pedro assured her. 'The Prince of the Peace has been unpopular for a very long time. I agree with His Royal Highness. If Your Majesties were to dismiss Godoy he would at least escape with his life.'

'Then he *is* in danger!' cried the Queen.

'It would seem so, Madam.'

'I cannot . . . I cannot dismiss him after all the services he has rendered to us,' said the King unhappily. 'That would be too ungrateful, and quite wrong – quite immoral.'

'A way could be found,' suggested Caballero. 'Your Majesty could, for instance, state that Godoy himself has asked you to relieve him of his duties . . . that you have agreed and that you yourself will take over the command of the army and navy.'

'Yes, yes, that sounds much better, doesn't it, Maria Luisa?' said the King.

'Before you sign anything, Charles,' the Queen told him, 'I want an assurance from Ferdinand, before the present witnesses. I want him to swear most solemnly that he will spare the life of the Prince of the Peace, that he will do everything in his power to find him, that he will not allow him to be harmed in any way whatsoever.'

'I swear, mother,' replied the Prince, 'that insofar as it is possible and in my power, I shall comply with your request.'

'You have heard, gentlemen?' asked the Queen, turning to the Minister and Secretary of State. They bowed gravely.

Half an hour later the royal proclamation was posted at
the palace gates. A roar went up from the crowds as the news
passed from mouth to mouth. 'Godoy has been dismissed!
Godoy has been dismissed! Long live the King!'

Charles, pale and shaking, stepped on to the balcony, faced
the delirious crowds and made a supreme effort to look
pleased at the ovation.

The Queen gripped Ferdinand by the arm. 'Where is
Manuel?' she asked him. 'You know where he is. I know you
do.'

Ferdinand shook his head. 'I swear, mother, I do *not* know
where he is.'

'Then it may be too late,' the Queen moaned. 'They must
have murdered him already. You have played on our feelings,
Ferdinand, you have tricked us.'

XXVI

Godoy himself had tricked everybody into believing that he
had escaped from his residence. After spending the night
inside the rolled-up carpets in his attic, exhausted by fatigue
and thirst, he crept out of his hiding-place in the early
morning of the 19 March and peered cautiously out of the
window. A picket was mounting guard in the garden. Godoy
put a hand up to his dry throat. His family and staff had left
the house. He would starve if he were to stay in the attic, and
who could foresee the mood of the crowds? He could hear
shouts in the distance; the insurgents were still patrolling the
town. At any moment they might return and set fire to his
house. The prospect made him decide to risk creeping
downstairs to the store room. (This account is taken from his
own memoirs.)

The sentry on duty started and turned upon hearing the
floorboards creak; he was astounded to see Godoy standing
at the door, dishevelled, unshaven, shaking. 'For God's sake

give me a glass of water,' he begged the sentry hoarsely. The sentry rushed to the window and shouted to the picket: 'He's here! Godoy is here!'

With an exultant cry, the crowd rushed up the garden path like a pack of hounds. Godoy fell back against the wall, but he was quickly seized and dragged out. A jubilant cry came from the people pressed behind the iron railings: 'They have found him! They have found the traitor!'

Everybody flocked to rejoice at the spectacle of his humiliation and forced their way into the courtyard to spit at him and rain blows on his head and shoulders.

A group of soldiers rode up from the palace. 'There are strict orders from the Prince of Asturias,' they told the mob, 'not to harm Godoy. Leave him to us.' One of the soldiers plunged into the advancing crowds to ward them off. 'Give him a hat and a cloak to prevent him from being recognized and attacked,' he shouted.

Another soldier dismounted, ran into the house and found a cape and a wide-brimmed hat in the hall which he threw over Godoy, who was then pushed between two men on horseback; each one held him by the collar of the cape while he supported himself as best he could by the horses' bridles.

As he was marched through the streets the threatening crowds shouted for his blood. Men and women ran up to him from under and behind the horses' legs to shower blows upon him; one man jabbed him with a knife, another struck him across the mouth; he began to spit blood.

The Queen's servants hurried to the palace to inform their royal mistress of Godoy's painful progress. Half-crazed with terror, Maria Luisa flew to the King's study from where he had just dismissed Beauharnais, who had driven to Aranjuez in haste to find out what was happening. (Some historians have asserted that he had played an active role in the uprising.)

'Charles, Charles, they are killing Manuel!' the Queen cried wildly. 'Call Ferdinand at once. He promised that he would protect him.'

Ferdinand faced his distracted parents placidly. 'The people will not take orders from you any more, sire,' he told the King. 'They will only listen to me. You heard how they called for me last night and again today. I shall save Godoy's life if you agree to abdicate in my favour. You said only the other day, in the presence of witnesses, that you felt too weary to govern any more. You have always wished to lead a quiet life.'

'This is no time to argue. Manuel is in grave danger; we can discuss the details later. For God's sake go at once, Ferdinand, and rescue Manuel before they kill him,' the Queen implored him.

Godoy was in a sorry plight when Ferdinand confronted him in the guard's room to which he had been confined after his rough passage through the town. He fell at the Prince's feet crying: 'I beg forgiveness of Your Majesty. I presume that you are now the King?'

'Not yet, Manuel,' said the Prince, 'but I soon shall be.'

'Then may Your Royal Highness pardon my offences.'

Ferdinand looked down at the bleeding, bloated face upturned to his; he must have recalled the visit that Godoy had paid him in his prison at the Escorial. Who could have imagined that their roles would be so quickly reversed? For the first and only time in his life, Ferdinand behaved regally.

'Manuel,' he murmured gently and with dignity, 'the wrongs I have received at your hands are forgiven you, but Spain has an account to settle with you for the harm that you have done to her.'

The Prince then turned, climbed on to the sill of the barred window overlooking the square, and addressed the crowds gathered outside: 'Gentlemen, I answer for this man. He shall be tried, and his punishment will fit the gravity of his crimes.'

Cheering crowds accompanied the Prince back to the palace, which they continued to surround expectantly in anticipation of the news that everybody was hoping for. They had not long to wait.

That evening, at 7 p.m., in the presence of his ministers and councillors, King Charles IV of Spain removed the diadem from his head, placed it on that of Ferdinand, and signed a formal abdication in his favour:

As my habitual infirmities no longer permit me to carry the heavy burden of governing my kingdom, and needing, for the sake of my health, to lead a life of retirement in a more temperate climate, I have decided – after the fullest consideration – to abdicate in favour of my beloved son Ferdinand, Prince of Asturias.

One of Ferdinand's first acts as King was to give orders for Godoy to be escorted to Madrid to await trial. He was taken to the village of Pinto, outside the capital, for fear the mob might lynch him. Then Ferdinand asked the Dukes of Hijar and Montijo to return to Madrid with their henchmen and prevent any further disturbance. It was rumoured that Murat, Grand Duke of Berg, was rapidly approaching with his troops.

The ragged mob wandered slowly back to their respective homes and hovels, well pleased with their role in the uprising of Aranjuez.

XXVII

Inside the palace, relations between the members of the royal family had never been so strained. Ferdinand strutted about issuing decrees for the distribution of alms in the suburbs of Madrid, the lowering of the price of tobacco, and permits to hunt in the royal parks which were also to be reduced in size so as to give the people more pastures. The Duke of Infantado was recalled from his exile and Urquijo was freed in Bilbao.

The King had already repented his abdication and his daughter Luisetta upbraided him for his spinelessness. The

Queen agreed. She was frantic with fear for her beloved Manuel, about whom she had heard nothing, and she mistrusted Ferdinand.

Luisetta had been on good terms with Murat. He had greeted her and her late husband when they arrived in Florence to take up their transient abode there as Kings of Etruria; she had met him again recently in Milan and he had always been gallant. Could she not appeal to him personally for help? She wrote him a letter which was entrusted to a courier disguised as a market gardener; the letter was hidden among the vegetables in the panniers of his mule.

In the meantime Beauharnais informed Ferdinand that it was possible the Emperor would pay a visit to Spain. The Prince was delighted. He would be able to discuss all pending questions verbally and meet the great man face to face at last. He planned a royal entry into Madrid where he would make the acquaintance of Murat, who was stationed near the capital at El Molar.

Murat received the ex-Queen of Etruria's letter as he was getting ready for his own entry into Madrid. He intended this to be a flamboyant spectacle, in accordance with his taste and temperament. He chose his accoutrement with care: a green velvet jacket, red leather boots, a red silk sash. Finally he stuck a magnificent white plume into his long, raven black hair. People gaped admiringly as he set out at the head of his handsome, well-polished carabiniers, cuirassiers, hussars and turbaned Turkish mamelouks.

Murat had been waiting impatiently for instructions from the Emperor. Meanwhile, on the basis of the news from Aranjuez and Luisetta's appeal, he decided to turn the bickerings within the royal family to his advantage. Ferdinand, he believed, was only a pawn, inexperienced and incapable of governing. Surely Napoleon would wish to give the crown to a French successor – to a member of his family . . . Why not to him, Murat?

Before leaving for Madrid, Murat sent his aide-de-camp General Monthion to Aranjuez for a personal interview with The Kings and Luisetta to confirm his opinion of the recent events and help him to work out a plan.

General Monthion reached the palace of Aranjuez at eight o'clock in the morning of 23 March. At that early hour, and after so many late and sleepless nights, nobody in the royal palace was astir. Luisetta, for whom the General carried a letter from Murat, was still in bed. Her servants asked the General to wait in the ante-room while she hurriedly dressed.

After reading Murat's letter Luisetta communicated the contents to her parents. Half an hour later the three of them came in together and the King advanced, smiling, to greet the General.

'How grateful we are to his Highness,' said Charles effusively, 'for taking an interest in our misfortune – a misfortune all the more painful to bear for having been brought about by our own son.'

The Queen interjected bitterly: 'The uprising was planned by Ferdinand's partisans, particularly Caballero, the Minister of Justice. Justice! Is that not ironical? The crowds were bribed. It was a shameful affair.'

'I was forced to abdicate,' the King assured the General, 'in order to save my life and that of the Queen; otherwise we would both have been murdered during the night.'

'You may well look astonished,' said the Queen, 'but such are the depths to which a depraved character can descend. The Prince of Asturias wants us to retire to Badajoz near the Portuguese frontier; we have pointed out to him that the climate would not suit His Majesty. Nevertheless he insists upon sending us there next Monday. Can this be prevented?'

'Our only wish,' explained the King wearily, 'is to obtain permission from His Imperial Majesty to acquire a property in France where we may spend the rest of our lives in peace and tranquillity.'

'With the Prince of the Peace – if he is still alive,' added the Queen.

'Oh yes, with the Prince of the Peace,' the King echoed
eagerly. 'I am — we are — deeply grieved and disturbed on his
account. He has been removed from us and we fear for his
life.'

The Queen turned her head to hide her tears.

'His only crime is that of having served us faithfully for
twenty years. I beg of you to inform the Emperor — I
implore His Imperial Majesty to set the poor Prince of the
Peace at liberty. He has always been the friend of France,'
said the King.

'May the Grand Duke of Berg obtain from the Emperor
the wherewithal on which the King my husband, myself and
the Prince of the Peace can live, all three of us, in some place
that will suit our health, far removed from intrigues,' the
Queen beseeched the General.

'The Grand Duke will no doubt wish to see these
sentiments expressed in a letter to the Emperor,' the General
suggested.

'Of course, of course. We shall write straight away,' said
the Queen, adding: 'Did the Grand Duke have any particular
suggestions to make with respect to our plea? How do you
thing he would like us to draft it?'

Murat had been most explicit and the General saw to it
that the King's letter was phrased according to his instructions. He had even made a rough draft of what he
thought The Kings should write to Napoleon. Charles wrote
obediently:

I have been compelled to abdicate but now, placing my entire
confidence in the magnanimity of the great man who has always shown
himself to be my friend, I have resolved to acquiesce with whatever he
may decide as to my future, that of the Queen and of the Prince of the
Peace. I hereby make a solemn protest against the procedure adopted at
Aranjuez and against my forced abdication.

It was agreed that this letter would be ante-dated 20
March, the day after the abdication. Well satisfied with the
result of his mission General Monthion took his leave.

'I trust that you will continue to be our liaison officer,'

said Luisetta, 'between the Grand Duke of Berg, my parents and myself. I propose to leave for Madrid tomorrow and to take up residence in the palace. From there I shall be in a position to report on my brother's actions to the Grand Duke, whom I hope to meet again soon.'

Murat was flattered by the reception given to him in Madrid; the populace acclaimed his dazzling arrival with enthusiastic cries of: 'Long live Napoleon! Death to Godoy!' They appeared to be under the impression that the French would help to rid them of their arch-enemy and they were pleased when Murat installed himself in the favourite's ex-residence near the royal palace. The mob had invaded it as soon as they had heard he had been made prisoner. They had slashed Goya's medallions in the main staircase – those which had been admired by Lucien Bonaparte during his brief ambassadorship – but otherwise they had behaved with restraint. Nothing had been stolen. The great artist himself who, ever since the death of the Duchess of Alba in 1802 and his increasing deafness, had immured himself in his Casa del Sordo was wheedled out of his retreat by the newly-appointed members of Ferdinand's Council of State to paint a portrait of Ferdinand as King.

'Your Majesty,' Murat wrote smugly to Napoleon, the night of 23 March, after describing his triumphal entry into the capital, 'with these troops and cannons I am ready for anything!'

On the following day Ferdinand made his entry into Madrid riding on a white horse followed by a carriage containing his uncle Don Antonio and his brother Carlos. They were received with frenzied acclamations of *'Viva el Rey!'* Capes, mantillas, flowers were thrown under the horses' hooves. Church bells pealed and rockets were fired as the King was finally borne on a human tide into his palace from where he immediately sent for the Duke of Infantado and Canon Escoiquiz. The Duke de Pague was sent to Murat to announce Ferdinand's arrival and the Duke of Medinaceli, Counts Frais

and Fernan-Nuñez were sent to France to announce the news
of the accession to Napoleon whom, it was believed, they
might meet on his way to Spain.

Murat, on his side, wrote to Napoleon on 24 March to
inform him that he had been approached by Charles and he
proposed (what he had already accomplished) that the
ex-King should write a letter declaring that his abdication had
been forced upon him. He enclosed a draft of the letter
which he assured the Emperor the King would be ready to
sign in his present unfortunate circumstances. 'If – as all
presume – Ferdinand has obtained the abdication by force,'
Murat concluded, 'he will have to be treated as a rebel.'

Between 21 March and 20 April Murat was bombarded by
seventeen letters from the Queen, six from Luisetta and two
from Charles.

Maria Luisa begged Luisetta over and over again to explain
to the Grand Duke of Berg the

position of my husband, myself and that of the poor Prince of the
Peace. My son Ferdinand was at the head of the conspiracy; the troops
had been won over to his side. He had lights placed in the window of
his room as a signal for the uprising to commence. At the same time
the guards and the leaders of the revolt fired shots into the air.
Ferdinand said they were the guards of the Prince of the Peace but that
is untrue. The King and I called Ferdinand to say that his father was in
pain, that he could not go to the window, that Ferdinand should do so
to calm the mob. He replied that he wouldn't because as soon as he did
so firing would start. Next morning we asked him if he could have the
tumult stopped; he said that he would and also that he would send the
people back to Madrid who had come to stir up trouble. Another
uprising had been planned for the 19th, the day on which there was a
plot against the life of my husband, and my own, so we were obliged to
take the decision to abdicate. Ferdinand has treated us with the utmost
contempt. My son is insensitive and not inclined to clemency. He is
advised by wicked men who are dominated by ambition. Ferdinand
makes promises but he does not keep them.

The Queen had laid down her cards. In the absence of
Godoy and her uncertainty about his fate she fulminated
against her son, denouncing him to their common enemy
with an utter lack of maternal feeling or patriotic decency.

'How is the Prince of the Peace? How is he being treated? Spare him — free him — ' she wrote hysterically.

PART SIX

THE TRAP IS SET

XXVIII

News of the Aranjuez uprising and Charles's subsequent abdication reached Napoleon at St Cloud on the Saturday evening of 26 March, the day after he had sent Tournon back to Spain for a further report; he did not trust his boastful brother-in-law, Murat, whose ambitions he had reason to suspect.

It was remarked by his entourage that the Emperor looked worried when he attended Sunday morning Mass. After his customary rapid luncheon, the Emperor called for General Savary (later to receive the title of Duke of Rovigo) and walked him round the park for two hours. 'Savary would kill his own father if I asked him to,' Napoleon once told his Chief of Police Fouché. Savary was one of the few men he could trust implicitly.

'You are to leave for Madrid tomorrow,' Napoleon told him. 'I have heard that King Charles IV has abdicated and that his son has succeeded him. This occurred during a revolution which appears to have toppled Godoy, and it inclines me to believe that the King's abdication has not been effected of his own free will. I was prepared for changes in Spain but from the turn which events have taken they are following a path which I had not foreseen. Have a word with our ambassador and tell me what role he has played in these events. Find out why he did not prevent a revolution which will not fail to be imputed to me and in which I am forced to intervene. Before recognizing the son, I want to know exactly what his father's sentiments are, for it is he who is my ally. It is with him that I have a treaty and if he asks for my support I shall give it to him unreservedly and will re-instate him on the throne in spite of all the intrigues. I now see that he was right to accuse his son of plotting against him. Recent events confirm it. I shall never approve of such an action – it would dishonour my policy and would one day turn against me. But if the abdication of the father was voluntary and has been accomplished without violence, then I shall see whether I can reach an agreement with the son . . .

'When Charles V abdicated he was not only content with a written declaration to that effect, he proved and stressed its authenticity by following a ceremonial appropriate to the occasion and this more than once. In the absence of a proper legal procedure, any band of traitors could introduce themselves into my apartments one fine night, make me abdicate and overthrow the entire state. If the Prince of Asturias is to reign, I must know him. I must find out whether he is capable of governing by himself and if so what his policy is and whether I can remain on the same footing with him as I was with his father. I do not think that this will be the case for revolutions are caused by extremes and one of the new King's means of gaining popularity will have been his avowed intention of following a different policy from that of his father who himself caused me some concern after Jena.

'I fear a Spanish alliance with England. I have everything to fear from a revolution of which I know neither the purpose nor the means by which it occurred. It would be better to avoid a war with Spain. This would be almost a sacrilege — but I would not hesitate to wage war on the House of Bourbon if the Prince who governs Spain adopts a hostile attitude. I shall then find myself in a similar position to that of Louis XIV when that sovereign dealt with the succession of Charles II. It was said that he had been prompted by ambition, but it was not so; if he had not placed one of his grandsons on the throne of Spain an Austrian archduke would have taken it; then Spain would have become England's ally and Louis XIV would have had to wage war on two fronts. If Spain is governed by a hostile Prince he might one day take it into his head to restore the throne of France to his family. Imagine what would happen to France in such an event! If I cannot reach an agreement with the father or with the son I shall assemble the *Cortes* and begin the work of Louis XIV all over again. I am prepared to do this. I am leaving for Bayonne. If circumstances compel me to I shall go to Madrid, but I shall not do that unless I am absolutely forced to.'

On his return to the palace of St Cloud after his conversation with Savary, the Emperor wrote to his brother Louis, King of Holland, offering him the crown of Spain, as if he were already the master of that country. His tactless letter wounded Louis deeply.

The King of Spain has abdicated. The Prince of the Peace is in prison. An insurrection has broken out in Madrid. While all this was taking place my troops were forty leagues away from the capital, but the Grand Duke of Berg should have entered it by now with 40,000 men. The people have been loud in their appeals to me throughout the crisis. Convinced as I am that there will never be lasting peace with England until I put the whole of Europe in motion, I have determined to put a French prince on the throne of Spain. The Dutch climate does not suit you; Holland can never rise again from its ashes. Things being so, I am thinking of you for the throne of Spain. There you will be sovereign of a generous nation of eleven million souls with important colonies overseas. Given the necessary impetus, economy and drive, Spain might have 60,000 men under arms and fifty warships in its ports. Don't take anyone into your confidence, answer yes or no.

Louis, piqued by the implication that he had been placed knowingly at the head of an unhealthy, uneconomic kingdom, replied haughtily: 'No. I am not the governor of a province.' The Emperor then turned to his reluctant brother Joseph in Naples.

On 29 March Napoleon began paving his way to the disparagement of the new King of Spain by having an article published by *Le Moniteur* against Ferdinand and the 'revolting intrigues and perfidy of the ministers who had engineered the uprising of Aranjuez', which gave to understand that Charles's abdication had been forced upon him.

XXIX

General Savary had set out for Madrid on 27 March. At almost every one of his halts he crossed couriers on their way to Paris with dispatches from Ferdinand to his newly-appointed ambassador. At Poitiers Savary met the Count of Fernan-Nuñez, the palace chamberlain, with a message from Ferdinand to the Emperor; at Bayonne he saw the Infante Don Carlos, who had been sent to greet the Emperor.

Throughout the province of Biscay triumphal arches had been set up for the expected passage of Napoleon. Cries of 'Long live Napoleon! Down with Godoy!' rose from all sides as if the victory of the one would spell disaster for the other.

At Vitoria, the General was surprised to be saluted by a French officer dispatched by Murat to the Emperor, carrying the sword which had belonged to Francis I of France and kept as a war trophy since his defeat at the battle of Pavia in 1525 by the royal armoury of Madrid. 'This sword,' General Savary observed in his memoirs, 'could have been claimed a hundred years earlier by Louis XIV, but the latter wisely considered that it did not behove him to insult a nation by robbing it of one of its most glorious mementoes.'

The removal of Francis I's sword, which had taken place on 31 March, was the first of Murat's *faux pas* in Spain and one which roused the population of Madrid against him. Murat was too cocksure, surrounded as he was by well organized troops, aware that Ferdinand, whom he studiously avoided addressing as King, only disposed of 3,000 men and was being advised by an inexperienced coterie of amateur ministers united in a council presided over by the Infante Don Antonio.

Even so, Murat should have realized that to ask for Francis I's sword only a week after his entry into Madrid would not make him popular, all the more so since he turned the event into a solemn occasion. He had a fine carriage escorted by hussars sent to the royal armoury next to the palace; the sword was placed on a raised dais covered with red velvet and taken at a slow pace through the streets of the capital for all to see. Yet after this he was capable of writing such inanities to Napoleon as: 'Ferdinand is losing favour with the people daily' – 'Your Imperial Majesty is awaited here like the Messiah.'

Canon Escoiquiz, who had arrived in Madrid, was made a member of Ferdinand's Council of State. The Queen, who was now at the Escorial with Charles under French protection, warned Murat against 'that wicked hypocrite of a cleric, Escoiquiz'. When the Canon called upon Murat to sound his intentions vis à vis his royal master, Murat found him 'frank, witty and intelligent'. He agreed with the Queen's assessment of her brother-in-law Don Antonio when she told him 'his talents are very limited and he has a very weak character', but he could not believe, as the Queen assured him, that the little Infante was 'bloodthirsty' to boot. Ferdinand too, the Queen wrote acrimoniously in her general condemnation of her family, 'is bloodthirsty. He has never felt any affection for his father or for me, he has inflamed the people against us because we are the allies of the French; my son is false – he refers with contempt to the French troops.'

Still half-crazed with fear of what might befall her favourite, she wrote wildly: 'They will have Godoy beheaded in public and then it will be our turn because that is what they are saying; my son is very coldhearted and he has no feelings whatsoever.'

In the absence of precise instructions from Paris, Murat could not commit himself to acknowledging Ferdinand as King, although Canon Escoiquiz assured him of his friendship and even asked him for advice as to the future, no doubt in order to ascertain what Murat and the Emperor intended to do about Spain. Murat replied evasively; he had assured Charles that he would not recognize anyone else but him as the legitimate sovereign.

And then, much to Murat's annoyance, General Savary arrived in Madrid as the Emperor's special envoy with the delicate mission of making friends with both Beauharnais and Murat, who were at loggerheads, and of persuading Ferdinand to have a face to face interview with the Emperor. It was Savary's secret mission, although he continued to deny this even in his memoirs, to lure Ferdinand step by step to the mousetrap of Bayonne. Savary was to play the role of the enticing piece of cheese. He assured everybody concerned, however, that he had been sent to Madrid only to investigate the situation in view of the conflicting reports that had reached the Emperor.

Beauharnais greeted Savary with relief for he was at his wits' end, in the absence of a letter of credentials from the Emperor, to know what to answer to repeated queries and visits from Escoiquiz on behalf of Ferdinand and the Council of State as to why Ferdinand was not being acknowledged as King. On the other hand Murat treated Beauharnais with scant respect. He had never liked Josephine and her relations.

During one of his interviews with Beauharnais the Canon was introduced to Savary who affected to be impressed by the Canon's devotion to Ferdinand; the latter wept openly as he expressed his fear of 'seeing his royal master made unhappy. The King desires nothing better than to be on good terms with France,' the Canon assured Savary.

The General replied that appearances gave a very different impression. Escoiquiz reaffirmed Ferdinand's feelings of friendship for the Emperor and complained that Murat was behaving very badly by avoiding him. Escoiquiz then returned to the palace to report on his interview while Savary waited for the result.

Soon afterwards the Duke of Infantado, who had conferred with Ferdinand after listening to Escoiquiz, called upon Savary to ask him whether he would like to see the King. Savary stressed that he had not been sent on any mission; he had merely come to Madrid as an observer to ascertain the facts.

'But,' the Duke insisted, 'it would be useful if you were to hear from the King's own lips how well he thinks of France and how friendly he feels towards your Emperor.'

Savary had at last achieved his carefully concealed objective. He was about to be introduced to Ferdinand and the suggestion had come from the King himself. There remained the difficulty of court protocol, raised by Infantado.

'How will you address the King?' he asked arrogantly.

'What do you mean?' Savary feigned innocence.

'I mean, do you intend to address him as Your Majesty?'

Savary attempted to pass the matter off lightly. 'This is a child's game; however I address your master it signifies nothing since I have no credentials.'

But in order to see Ferdinand he agreed to address him as 'Majesty' and was finally ushered into the royal apartments where he spoke with Ferdinand, Escoiquiz, the Duke of San Carlos and Don Pedro Cevallos.

Savary again insisted that he had not been charged with a specific mission but Ferdinand interrupted him to exclaim: 'We have no grudge against France but we have been led to believe that you wish to protect the Prince of the Peace and that is none of your business. Murat asks daily for his release on behalf of my father and mother.'

Savary did not wish to quarrel over this issue so he replied cautiously: 'Until Your Majesty is recognized by the Emperor we must fulfil our engagements with the King your father who has placed himself under our protection.'

Both Escoiquiz and the Duke of San Carlos rejoined in chorus: 'We wish to have even better relations with the Emperor than the late King had.'

'I believe you, gentlemen,' answered Savary, 'but in that case the facts must tally with your assurances. The Emperor takes an interest in all that is happening in Spain. He is himself approaching the frontier and will probably come as far as Madrid. I believe that he must have already left Paris. He will receive my dispatches en route. You must realize that he will not want to take sides until he has discussed the situation with Charles IV.'

Savary left Ferdinand and his suite in a state of considerable perplexity; this was part of his stratagem. The thought that Napoleon wanted to have a frank discussion with Charles would prompt Ferdinand, so he hoped, to be the first to meet the Emperor. In subsequent conversations at the palace Savary pressed this point which began to be discussed openly. 'The Emperor would no doubt be flattered were the new King to meet him at some point on his way to Madrid, say at Burgos.'

Canon Escoiquiz believed, or so he wrote in his memoirs, that Ferdinand had made a grave mistake in coming to Madrid, and that he should have remained at Aranjuez with his troops, from where, if pressed, he could have retreated with The Kings and Godoy to the south of Spain and there assembled forces to oppose Napoleon. This was the same course of action which Godoy had wanted finally to take. Things being what they were, however, the Canon took another line.

XXX

On 6 April Ferdinand had a further meeting with his counsellors.

'General Savary called on me again this morning privately,' Ferdinand told them, 'and pressed me more urgently than ever to expedite a direct confrontation with the Emperor to clarify my position. He says that Napoleon is anxious to make my acquaintance.'

'I am ready to believe that,' interjected Don Pedro Cevallos; 'so far he had heard the most contradictory reports about Your Majesty. The poison poured into his ears by we all know who is bound to have produced some effect. It is natural to suppose that he is in a quandary.'

O'Farill, the Minister of War, a blunt, bluff man, laughed scornfully. 'Quandary? Why? Facts are facts. His Majesty Ferdinand VII is now the legitimate King of Spain. How is it then that neither the Grand Duke of Berg, who must receive instructions from Napoleon daily, nor the French ambassador in Madrid, who at one time was so ready to assist His Majesty, now avoid him and refuse to address him by his correct title? In my view this bodes no good.'

'All the more reason,' said the Canon, 'for His Majesty to comply with General Savary's request and have talks with Napoleon. In my opinion it is of the utmost urgency before the situation deteriorates still further.'

'It is deteriorating,' Ferdinand agreed. 'The populace is restless and becoming daily more hostile towards the French troops in the capital. That is why we have organized nightly patrols in every quarter of Madrid so as to prevent clashes.'

'There are too many French troops in the capital,' muttered the Duke of Infantado. 'I don't like it. I suspect that the Grand Duke of Berg is taking measures of which the Emperor would disapprove. He is a very ambitious and haughty man.'

'He is also on very friendly terms with the ex-Queen of Etruria,' remarked the Canon pointedly.

'And with my august parents,' said Ferdinand. 'We all know, as we have informed General Savary, although he too must be aware of it, that my parents clamour for Godoy's release through the intermediary of my sister Luisetta.'

'His guardian the Marquis of Castelar says that he wouldn't be surprised if his prisoner were to be snatched from under his nose one of these days or nights,' said the Marquis of Olaguer.

'Oh come, the Grand Duke would not dare to go that far,' began the Duke of San Carlos.

The Duke of Olaguer shook his head. 'I would not be so sure, gentlemen. It looks very much as if their ex-Majesties and the ex-Queen of Etruria have won the Grand Duke of Berg over to their side. No doubt they will have written to the Emperor too.'

'He has no time for Godoy, surely,' said Ferdinand. 'He will never support a man whom he knows is detested by the whole of Spain. We must not exaggerate Godoy's importance. That chapter is closed.'

'Nevertheless,' the Canon broke in, 'at the moment the Emperor is being assailed by pleas from their ex-Majesties who are supported by the Grand Duke, and he hears nothing from you, Your Majesty.'

'But I *have* written to him!' Ferdinand exclaimed. 'And he has not replied.'

'That seems ominous,' said the Canon. 'It is possible, as Savary has suggested, that your parents are planning to meet the Emperor themselves on his way to Madrid and so be the first to present their case. The Grand Duke would no doubt facilitate such an encounter. God knows what lies your parents are prepared to tell in order to obtain the release of Godoy! For that reason only I would strongly advise Your Majesty to set out immediately so as to precede them.'

Ferdinand thought that this was a good argument in favour of his leaving the capital but Olaguer was unconvinced. He pointed out that the last dispatch from Izquierdo to Godoy, dated 24 March, sent at a time when he believed that Godoy had left for the south with The Kings, contained a grave warning since 'he states that the Emperor wishes to conclude a new treaty with Spain which would deprive us of all our territories between the Ebro and the Pyrenees. This, gentlemen, is an impossible demand which must be resisted.' (As we know, Godoy too had been opposed to this cession of territory.)

'It should not be taken too seriously,' the Canon interrupted. 'Napoleon wants a free passage to Portugal for his troops. It would only be a temporary measure, but of course that must be discussed verbally. I cannot urge you too strongly, Your Majesty, to meet the Emperor as soon as you can. Any delay is a sign of vacillation and weakness on our part.'

O'Farill, seconded by Canon Escoiquiz, suggested that before seeing Napoleon Ferdinand should try to obtain a letter from Charles to the effect that his son was as anxious as his father had always been to be friendly with the Emperor. Such a letter would prove that father and son were in agreement. Accordingly, on 8 April, Ferdinand wrote:

My revered father, General Savary has just left me. I am very pleased with our interview. I like him very much. He says that the Emperor entertains the friendliest feelings towards me, and I wish to continue on the same footing as you were.

He then proceeded to ask his father for a confirmation of this in writing. The Queen saw through the stratagem at once and was all in favour of sending a sarcastic reply but Murat assured her that this would serve no good purpose and he kept the letter back. It might, he thought, come in useful later as evidence of the hopeless tangle in which the royal family found itself.

The pawns in this game of political chess had now reached stalemate. A move had to be made. The Kings continued to pester Murat from their hide-out at the Escorial, Luisetta ex-Queen of Etruria intrigued with Murat from her apartments in the palace of Madrid, while Ferdinand argued with his ministers in his. Murat was on bad terms with Beauharnais and both of them were at sea as far as their imperial master's plans were concerned. Godoy languished in gaol, incommunicado and uncertain of his fate. Incidents occurred daily between the Spaniards and the French troops stationed in Madrid.

On 8 April Ferdinand gave in to the combined pressure of General Savary and of his ministers. He wrote to Napoleon informing him that he was setting out from the capital to meet him at Burgos. The members of his council entreated him earnestly not to venture beyond that point until he had received a satisfactory reply from the Emperor.

A notice was published in the official gazette of 9 April 1808 to the effect that the King, having been informed through a reliable source that his august ally the Emperor of France and King of Italy was on the point of arriving at Bayonne with the intention of pursuing his journey to Madrid, had decided to leave the capital to meet him and assure him of his desire to maintain their firm alliance.

In his absence, which would only last several days, his people of Madrid were enjoined to obey the orders of the Junta established in the palace under the presidency of the Infante Don Antonio, which included the Ministers of the Interior, Azanza, of War, O'Farill, of Justice, Caballero, and of the Navy, Gil.

PART SEVEN

THE TRAP CLOSES

XXXI

On 10 April Ferdinand left Madrid accompanied by the Dukes of Infantado, San Carlos, the Marquis of Ayerbe, Don Pedro Cevallos, and Canon Escoiquiz (whose knowledge of French was superior to that of the King and his friends). General Savary was placed in a carriage behind that of the King. All of them, with the exception of the General, were confident of meeting the Emperor at Burgos, 168 miles from the frontier, and they looked out expectantly when the two great Gothic towers of the cathedral came into view on the third day of their journey. They had stopped at Buitraga on the first night and at Aranda del Duero on the second.

The little grey town of Burgos was full of French troops, but the Emperor was not there and nobody had had any news of his whereabouts.

'Perhaps,' suggested General Savary suavely, the day after Ferdinand's arrival, 'the Emperor has only just crossed the frontier and is on his way to Vitoria. Could we not drive on? It is only seventy-one miles from Burgos.' Only a little closer to the mousetrap . . .

The King showed signs of reluctance but his entourage persuaded him to proceed. There was bound to be news of the Emperor at Vitoria . . .

Count Tournon-Simiane, who was at Burgos at the time, sent the Emperor a last perceptive dispatch. In his considered opinion, he wrote, judging from all that he had observed and heard during his exploratory mission,

the Spanish nation is unlike any other and one can only judge it from within. I consider it most important that you should decide to come here as quickly as possible and not to make any resolution until you have seen things for yourself. The Spaniards possess a noble and generous character but tend towards ferocity and would not bear to be treated as a conquered nation. Reduced to despair, they would be capable of the greatest and bravest revolutions and most violent excesses.

These prophetic words were written too late and went unheeded. Napoleon had made up his mind.

Talleyrand wrote in his memoirs that Napoleon spoke to him on several occasions about his plans to take over Spain, which he opposed as 'immoral and dangerous'. Napoleon insisted that any hostile move from Spain, should he meet with reverses on the banks of the Rhine or in Italy, would be highly dangerous; he reminded Talleyrand, in support of his contention, of Godoy's proclamation on the eve of the battle of Jena. Talleyrand rejoined that it was unjust to hold an entire nation responsible for the actions of one man whom it detested anyway and whose downfall had now been brought about. The Emperor objected that Godoy's example might be followed by others and that he did not feel safe on the Pyrenean frontier. Talleyrand then advised him to occupy Catalonia until he obtained a naval peace with England.

'You will declare to Spain that you will keep your pledge until the peace and by so doing you will hold the Spanish government in check. If the peace should be deferred, it is possible that Catalonia, which is the least Spanish of all the provinces of Spain, might become attached to France; there are historic traditions for this and perhaps one day Catalonia might become permanently united to France. Anything beyond that would cause you regrets.'

Talleyrand did not succeed in convincing the Emperor, who distrusted his wily Great Chamberlain's opinion on the Spanish issue and sensed that he was slipping farther and farther away from him.

The royal cortège set off for Vitoria, the coaches jolting slowly up the stony winding roads; green hills began to appear, their summits shrouded in northern mists. There was a sharp nip in the air. Red-nosed peasants stood and stared unbelievingly at the liveried carriages. Many of the people were blue-eyed descendants of Goth and Celt and Vandal, mountaineers full of fighting spirit and independent character. There was not one Spanish uniform in sight. Every sentry post at which the royal coaches drew up was filled with French soldiers. Ferdinand was already virtually a prisoner.

In the little mountain town of Vitoria, capital of Alava, the most prosperous of the Basque provinces, the French troops had been confined to quarters to avoid trouble with the local inhabitants who, more clear-sighted than their leaders, were alarmed to see their new King driving recklessly into the arms of the French. Even Ferdinand and his followers were suspicious when they were told that even here there was no sign or news of the Emperor and still no reply to the letter sent from Madrid.

The royal party lodged in a house in the colonnaded square. Canon Escoiquiz, who had caught a heavy cold, took to bed and was too ill to receive a visitor who had asked to see him on urgent business. This visitor was the ex-Minister Urquijo whom Ferdinand had freed from prison in Bilbao and now received graciously. He was invited to dinner and Urquijo took the opportunity to employ all his powers of persuasion to dissuade the King from falling into what he rightly believed to be a carefully prepared trap. He recounted the conversation later in a letter to a friend.

'Your Majesty,' he said in a voice trembling with emotion, 'the French gazettes have reported the Aranjuez rising in a most tendentious manner which reveals the Emperor's true designs. My firm belief is that Napoleon's objective is to suppress the reigning dynasty of Spain which is an obstacle to his imperial aspirations. He has filled Spain with his troops, as you have seen on your way here; in this very town of Vitoria you and your friends are in a prison guarded by General Savary. What is the object of your journey? How can a sovereign of Spain and the Indies submit to such an indignity? You are being lured to a foreign country without a proper invitation, without the etiquette observed on similar occasions and without having been recognized as King, since Your Majesty is still addressed by the French as the Prince of Asturias. Napoleon wishes to annex Spain.'

'Do you really think it is possible,' cried the Duke of Infantado, 'that a hero like Napoleon would disgrace himself by such a base action when the King is placing himself in his hands in good faith?'

'Your Grace,' rejoined Urquijo, 'read Plutarch; you will find that all the so-called Greek and Roman heroes acquired their reputation and glory by climbing over thousands of corpses ... Think too of the crowns that Charles V had removed, of his many cruelties and acts of perfidy; yet he is considered to be a great man and a hero. Have we not acted in a similar manner ourselves towards the Kings of the Americas and the Indies? Look closely at the origins of most of the world's dynasties, and what do you see? Murders, incest ... No, have no confidence in heroes, Your Grace! Do not allow His Majesty to take a step nearer France.'

'I still cannot see,' the Duke persisted, 'what motive could justify the conduct you attribute to Napoleon.'

'The French *Moniteur* is quite clear,' declared Urquijo. 'It states that the Emperor does not recognize the Prince as King, that his father's abdication, made under duress, is null and void. If Charles agrees with this view, as he may well be persuaded to do, and you pursue your journey as far as Bayonne, believe me neither he nor King Ferdinand will reign over Spain and the country will be plunged into a terrible disaster.'

'The whole of Europe, even France itself, would condemn such a course,' protested Ferdinand. 'Spain, with the assistance of England, could prove a formidable foe.'

'Forgive me, Your Majesty,' said Urquijo patiently, 'but those are illusions, vain illusions. Europe is impoverished and divided between the individual interests of its various components. If England came over to our side, our country would be reduced to the state of a battlefield between that country and France; we would be the losers. France? She would be proud to see her empire strengthened and extended and the thrones of Europe occupied by members of her beloved Emperor's family. The Bourbons of France, let me remind you, have been discredited. The French people welcome their liberation from their former oppressors. They would not be sorry to see the Bourbons removed from Spain. As for a possible Spanish resistance . . .' Urquijo shook his head sadly. 'Spain is like a Gothic building, made up of bits and pieces with as many different laws and customs as there are provinces; there is no such thing as national pride, no government capable of uniting all the disparate elements. Internal risings would only have the ultimate effect of enabling our colonies to free themselves from our dominion.'

'My dear friend, you are really much too pessimistic,' exclaimed the Duke of Infantado, who was a great admirer of France. 'If one were to believe all you say, our future is unrelievedly black and there is nothing we can do about it. I for one refuse to take so lubrigious a view. You are depressing us.'

'I am speaking to you as a patriot and a loyal subject of His Majesty,' Urquijo cried vehemently, 'and I therefore entreat you to put me and my views to the test. Send me to Bayonne as your emissary. Let me speak to Napoleon. In the meantime put a stop to this hazardous journey. Your Majesty, leave this town tonight, incognito. You can do this very easily through the house next door to the one in which you are staying, which has a secret underground passage. Señor Urbino, the mayor, who is a relative of mine, would facilitate your flight into Aragon. Once the Emperor hears that you are free he will be obliged to alter his plans.'

'What a romantic notion! His Majesty has no justification for taking to his heels in such an undignified manner!' The Duke of Infantado laughed indulgently and glanced at Ferdinand, who assented with a smile.

'Very well, Your Majesty – gentlemen. I shall say no more, but I fear that you will have cause to remember my warning when it is too late.' Urquijo concluded gloomily, as he rose to take his leave. 'I shall go back to my little corner while you hurry to your doom. I am sorry for Spain.'

'Dear me, what a Jeremiah!' exclaimed Ferdinand after he

had gone. 'He is a good man and he means well but he is too excitable and full of wild notions.'

Urquijo was not the only prophet of doom. Don José Hervas, son of the Spanish banker in Paris who dealt with the financial transactions between the two countries, and who had joined General Savary as an interpreter, sought out the Duke of Infantado and confirmed Urquijo's suspicions. Napoleon, said Hervas, was preparing to oust the Spanish dynasty. But his warnings, like those of Urquijo, were ignored.

Nevertheless, Ferdinand decided that he would go no further than Vitoria — at least not until he had heard from Napoleon.

When Don Pedro Cevallos informed General Savary of his decision, the latter objected that he could not see any reason for this change of plan. He had informed the Emperor of their itinerary and any alteration would give rise to false conjectures.

Canon Escoiquiz, who had now risen from his sickbed, could not conceal his uneasiness at the non-appearance of the Emperor. 'How unfortunate,' he exclaimed to Savary, 'if I and these gentlemen who wish to serve the King should be the cause of his ruin!'

To this Savary replied that he had received no communication from the Emperor since he had left Paris and he did not know what the Emperor had decided to do. 'But I believe, in all conscience,' he assured them, 'that he wishes above all things to avoid a war with Spain. I am personally convinced that he will form his opinions from what he learns and sees on the spot and that he will judge accordingly. All this depends on you. Do not attempt to deceive him; you know that that is no easy matter!'

'France has already interfered too much in our affairs,' Cevallos stated bluntly. 'There must be an end to it.'

The General then took a firmer line. 'That statement, Don Pedro, may be interpreted in several ways. Do you wish to dismiss me, or to take leave yourselves? Without being

The palace of La Granja, near Segovia, at the foot of the Guadarrama mountains, where the court spent part of the summer.

The gardens of La Granja, where Charles IV liked to turn the fountains on to unsuspecting visitors.

Goya's famous picture of the shootings following the people of
Madrid's uprising against the French, on 3 May 1808. It marked
the beginning of the Peninsular War.

In this room in the palace of Aranjuez Charles IV reluctantly signed his abdication in March 1808.

The royal palace of Madrid, and the coach still used for ambassadors presenting their credentials.

authorized to do so, I will take upon myself to accede to either of these alternatives and I will leave you gentlemen to answer for the consequences.'

'I do not see why the Emperor wishes to interfere in our affairs. Have we broken our alliance in any way?' Cevallos insisted. He was beginning to have grave doubts.

'The Emperor,' replied the General sternly, 'interferes in your affairs, as you put it, because they have become the affairs of France and closely connected with his interests. It does not matter to him who reigns in Spain if his relations with your country remain unimpaired. Finally, sir, you must either resist him, in which case he will make his own decisions as to what course to follow, or you must satisfy him, in which case you will not hesitate to give him a proof of your goodwill. Since you, Señor Cevallos, having once been attached to the Prince of the Peace, know better than any of these gentlemen present what the Emperor wishes, and you are aware of all our past relations with your country, I do not understand the objections you raise and cannot but infer that they conceal some nefarious design. Do you suspect us of bad faith towards the King? It is rather late to talk about being afraid, for in that case how do you justify having brought him here in the midst of our troops? Is he not under our guard and at our disposal? We have an infantry division in Vitoria, one at Briviesca and another in Burgos. If you wish to commence hostilities, tell me, where would you go? Do you intend to pursue the policy which Spain followed under Ferdinand's father? If you do, then why are you so alarmed? Why should the King be afraid to meet the Emperor and come to a better understanding with him?'

This strong language prompted Ferdinand to write a frank letter to Napoleon before continuing his journey. The General agreed to carry it to Bayonne in person.

'I shall tell the Emperor all that is to be feared as well as what is to be hoped for,' he observed cryptically before leaving Vitoria. 'He will surely send me back with his reply within two or three days.'

XXXII

Savary left his victims in a quandary and the local populace so agitated that Escoiquiz drafted a decree to calm them. History was repeating itself very soon. Charles had acted in a similar fashion at Aranjuez barely a month before.

The decree was nailed up in the main square.

The King is gratified by the demonstrations of affection shown by his loyal people of Alava but he regrets that it exceeds the proper limits. The King would not have undertaken his journey if he had not been assured of the sincerity and cordial friendship of the Emperor of the French and of its felicitous outcome.

For a moment Ferdinand and his entourage deliberated among themselves whether it would be expedient to attempt a last minute reconciliation with The Kings in order to make their negotiations with the Emperor easier and set his mind at rest about the legality of Charles's abdication. Azanza in Madrid had already suggested that a territory could be given to the Queen, to be hers alone and independent of Ferdinand in the event of Charles's death. Escoiquiz wrote to Azanza from Vitoria naming Don Joaquin Manuel as a possible intermediary. He also wrote to the Infante Don Antonio that Joaquin was to approach a member of Charles's household called Villena, and a sum of 20,000 reales was sent to him by Ferdinand and entered in his accounts. This item is the only tangible evidence, since no other documents have survived, of an obscure transaction undertaken too late to be followed up. In the circumstances, given the mood of The Kings, it is most unlikely that they would have considered the proposition for a single moment.

The church bells of the pretty Basque port of Bayonne were ringing joyously on the evening of 14 April 1808 even though it was Thursday in Holy Week when, from a strictly liturgical point of view, they should have been silent.

Orthodoxy, however, had been waived for the entry of the Emperor Napoleon, an extraordinary event for which the local authorities and inhabitants had made lavish preparations, insofar as their limited means permitted. Triumphal arches had been placed at the entrance to the town, the streets were decorated with evergreen branches, the citadel and public buildings were illuminated; the boats in the harbour were camouflaged under fluttering patterns of flags and bunting, fireworks had been ordered in unprecedented quantities.

As soon as the Emperor's coach was seen approaching on the road from Bordeaux cannons were fired from the fortress and from the ships in the harbour, while the Basque guard of honour, in festive uniform of blue berets, red jackets, white breeches and black gaiters, stood smartly to attention.

Government House, a cramped residence – Bayonne had nothing more impressive to offer – had been hastily refurnished for the Emperor's visit; the moment he arrived and set eyes upon it, he declared that it was not to his taste and far too small. He had noticed a more attractive building, the Château de Marrac, two miles outside the town. He gave orders for it to be bought, decorated and furnished within forty-eight hours. Nobody dared to object that this was impossible. A flustered army of builders, housepainters and carpenters were rushed out to Marrac and worked feverishly throughout the day and half the night, when the Emperor moved in.

The crowds were disappointed at the absence of the Empress Josephine from the Emperor's suite. She had been left behind at Bordeaux but it was said that she would soon be on her way and that the Château de Marrac was to be the centre of a brilliant social round of banquets and receptions; in brief, a miniature court.

Monsieur de Talleyrand, the Prince of Benevento, was also conspicuously absent. He was said to be indisposed. Those who knew better whispered that it was a diplomatic indisposition, that Monsieur de Talleyrand did not wish to take part in negotiations of which he disapproved; he guessed what was brewing in Napoleon's mind and what – despite the latter's apparent irresolution and contradictions – he had already made up his mind to do. It remained for the Emperor to accomplish the delicate feat of appearing to have his hand forced by events and by the characters in the drama for which the stage was being set.

When General Savary arrived in Bayonne with Ferdinand's anxious letter, the Emperor frowned and wondered for a moment whether it signified a setback to his plans. But he smiled confidently when he read the contents.

'The Prince,' he observed to the General, 'complains that after his father's voluntary abdication – ' the Emperor placed a sarcastic emphasis on the word 'voluntary' ' – I failed to instruct Beauharnais and Murat to recognize him as King. He tells me that he has demonstrated his good faith by ordering the return of the troops recalled from Portugal by the Prince of the Peace, by sending a deputation of grandees to welcome me, and by leaving the capital in person. He asks me to allay his anxiety by a favourable reply.

'Tell me, General, what sort of man is the Prince of Asturias? Does he govern or is he governed? In what manner do you think I can settle with him, or must I give up all hope of ever being able to do so? I am not inclined to adopt the latter course because it could lead to war.'

'Sire,' replied the General, 'I have had many assurances of Ferdinand's good intentions and as to promises, I have received pocketfuls, both from the Prince and from his ministers, but as to warranting their sincerity that I beg to be excused from doing.'

'There is no doubt in my mind,' Napoleon reflected aloud, 'that the Aranjuez revolution was contrary to Charles's wishes. This would be obvious were there no other proof than his alacrity to place him under the protection of our troops who, in fact, guard him at the palace of the Escorial at this very moment.'

The General nodded. 'On the other hand, sire, I do not think you will succeed in placing yourself on the same footing in Spain with Prince Ferdinand as with his father. The hope held out to his followers of throwing off the yoke of France has turned public opinion in his favour and made him so popular that to oppose him would be to oppose the entire nation. As to governing by himself, that he can never do. He has received a palace education and has not the slightest idea of what government entails. His ministers will be all powerful and they are unfriendly to us.'

Napoleon toyed with the pen which he had picked up to draft his reply to the Prince's letter. 'This looks bad. Matters went smoothly with his father. I used to pray he might live a hundred years, but if I must ultimately be embroiled with the son I shall not begin by doing that which he so anxiously desires. Why is he so afraid of me?'

'There are, I believe, several reasons: his own uncertain position, perhaps a feeling of self-reproach, his innate timidity, his fear of Murat and the latter's inclination to set the Prince of the Peace free. He thinks that Murat has received instructions to turn everybody against him.'

'Murat must be a fool to have given such an impression!'

'The Grand Duke of Berg, sire, appears to have taken it into his head that he will succeed the King of Spain himself.'

Napoleon laughed heartily.

'If Your Imperial Majesty does not give the Prince some token of security, he may decide not to come to Bayonne,' the General warned him.

'I shall consult my pillow, General, and give you my answer tomorrow.'

The next morning Napoleon handed General Savary a carefully worded letter for Ferdinand in which he adopted the paternalistic and slightly reproving tone of an older and wiser statesman — as he was:

The abdication of Charles IV took place at a time when my armies were in Spain and in the eyes of Europe it might appear that I had sent them with the sole object of driving my friend and ally from the throne. I must make myself fully acquainted with what has happened before I can recognize this abdication. If it was made of the King's own accord, I shall accept it and recognize Your Royal Highness as King of Spain. I wish to confer with you upon this subject.

When King Charles communicated to me the events of last October at the Escorial I was grievously affected and I consider that I contributed to its satisfactory solution. Your Royal Highness was then much at fault. The proof of this lies in the letter which you wrote to me and which it has been my constant desire to forget. When you become King you will learn how sacred are the rights of the throne. Any appeal made to a foreign sovereign by a Prince is criminal.

I am hesitating between various projects which will have to be settled between us. Believe in my sincere desire to compose all our differences . . .

'There,' said the Emperor to Savary, 'make all the haste you can, General, in delivering this letter to a Prince who, in a few days' time, will perhaps have ceased to reign or who will bring about a war between Spain and France.' He raised his eyes and exclaimed piously: 'Great Heavens, how nations are to be pitied when they fall into such hands!'

XXXIII

Upon his return to Vitoria, General Savary found the town full of armed peasants. Bessières told him that he had prevented an open battle by confining his troops to quarters.

Hurrying to the house in which the Prince and his suite were staying, the General stumbled over Spanish soldiers and men armed with poniards sprawling in the hall and on the stairs. He waited impatiently in the ante-room while Napoleon's reply was discussed by the Prince and his advisers.

After a few minutes Don Pedro Cevallos came out and expressed his master's dissatisfaction with the Emperor's use of the title 'Your Royal Highness' in his letter to the King. The General pointed out that the Emperor could not, with propriety, address him otherwise until the various questions to be settled between them had been fully discussed.

Then Ferdinand himself appeared in the doorway and the General added with a reassuring smile: 'I am ready to wager that a quarter of an hour after His Majesty's arrival at Bayonne, the Emperor will recognize him as King of Spain and the Indies. He will probably begin by calling you "Your Royal Highness"; five minutes later it will be "Your Majesty" and in three days everything will be settled and Your Majesty will be able to return to Spain.'

After this hypocritical assurance, and further deliberation between the Prince and his entourage, the latter resolved to take the final plunge and resume their journey to Bayonne the following day. They still could not bring themselves to believe that the Emperor would dupe them; it is possible, too, that they were secretly eager to set eyes upon the conqueror of Europe whom they regarded as a combination of ogre and father figure, not unlike Jehovah. They could not help themselves. They went to their ruin like lemmings.

Next morning, Cevallos sent a dispatch to the council in Madrid, signed by Ferdinand, advising them that the latter 'proposed to pay a visit to the Emperor in his country house of Marrac near the Spanish frontier, in response to his flattering invitation. He was leaving for Irún where he would spend the night before throwing himself into the arms of his distinguished friend. The King trusted that his faithful subjects would have confidence and that they would await his prompt return with calm.'

All was ready for the royal departure and the King was about to climb into his carriage when a tumult broke out. A fierce-looking peasant with a billhook in his hand pushed his way through the crowd, seized the traces of the eight mules harnessed to the royal carriage with one hand and with the other cut them at one stroke, at the point to which they were all attached.

'Bravo!' shouted the mob. *'Viva Fernando!* Do not leave us, Your Majesty — stay in Spain!'

'For God's sake,' cried the Duke of Infantado to Savary,

'get out of the way. Do not show your face to the crowd and do not allow your troops to show themselves either or there will be a riot and I cannot answer for the consequences. I shall do my best to quell it and have the mules brought back.'

An hour later, when the mob had realized the futility of their spontaneous gesture and saw that Ferdinand was determined to leave, they fell back and watched him depart in sorrowful silence. The man with the billhook, who had resisted every attempt to seize him, raised his arm defiantly in the direction of the royal carriage as it began to drive off towards France. 'If they so much as touch a hair of the King's head,' he roared, 'we shall avenge him. This billhook can cut off a Frenchman's head at one stroke just as it cut the mules' traces. You'll see if it can't!' It was not long before he would have the opportunity to put his threatening words into effect.

Ferdinand, who had travelled so little in his life, must have enjoyed the drive through the mountains. He had never before set his eyes on the Basque landscape and the Pyrenees. The foothills were covered with oaks, pines and larches and in the distance the snow-capped mountains sparkled in the early spring sunshine.

Soon the silvery-green Atlantic came into sight to the left and great foam-specked rollers slapping the golden sands of the Bidassoa estuary. On the edge of the torrential river that cascaded from the high mountain range lay the frontier post of Irún and immediately opposite the French town of Hendaye, joined by the bridge which had so often been crossed by Spanish Infantas and French princes in the course of political alliances.

Ferdinand was lodged in the house of a Señor Carrabal on the edge of the river, from where he sent a courteous note to the Emperor:

I intend to leave Irún tomorrow morning at 8 a.m. and hope to make the acquaintance of Your Imperial Majesty at Marrac, an event which I have been looking forward to for some time.

XXXIV

On 20 April the Prince crossed the narrow bridge over the Bidassoa and the wheels of his antiquated carriage rolled on-to French soil. Only twenty miles separated him from Bayonne, the Emperor and his unknown destiny. He was full of confidence and, as Canon Escoiquiz observed, gayer than he had ever been.

And then, only a few minutes later, came the first bombshell: two miles outside Bayonne the Infante Don Carlos and the deputation of grandees sent from Madrid on 2 April met the advancing royal party. The coaches stopped and the Infante and the Count of Frias got in to join the King.

The Count was the bearer of astounding news: in a conversation with the Emperor on the previous morning Napoleon had suddenly blurted out: 'The Bourbons must no longer reign in Spain.'

'But then why did you not send word to us?' cried Canon Escoiquiz. 'There was still time to stop us from crossing into France.'

'How could we? We didn't even know where you were,' replied the Count, who appeared to have completely lost his head.

'Everybody in Irún knew where we were lodging. If you had sent a message to us we could have escaped by Fuenterrabia in a fishing boat,' the Canon wailed.

'How could we have done that without being seen and overtaken? There are French troops and spies everywhere,' said Ferdinand disconsolately.

'If only we had known, we would never have come!' said the Canon.

'We have been in a state of stupor ever since the Emperor made that incredible statement. We were completely taken by surprise,' the Count assured Ferdinand.

Their conversation was interrupted by the French reception committee sent by Napoleon to greet Ferdinand and his party and escort them to to their residence, the Hotel Dubrocq – a low building with small windows which had belonged to the governor in the pre-revolutionary days. Bayonne did not possess princely residences. Cevallos, unaware of this fact, for the smallest Spanish town was full of houses adorned with armorial bearings, felt that they had been slighted. It was hardly the moment for a display of Castilian pique.

Ferdinand, repressing his anxiety, jumped down from his carriage and introduced his suite to the French reception committee which was composed of the Prince of Neuchatel, the Duke of Frioul and the Count d'Aubusson.

The Emperor was presiding over military manoeuvres on the esplanade in front of the citadel when an envoy rode up to tell him that Ferdinand had arrived in Bayonne. Napoleon gave orders for the exercises to be continued and then rode down to the Hotel Dubrocq, accompanied by an aide-de-camp and three gendarmes. Ferdinand advanced and impulsively threw his arms round the Emperor's shoulders, kissing him on both cheeks in the Spanish manner. Embarrassed by this effusion, Napoleon, tricorne in hand, turned his right and then his left cheek to the Prince who, addressing him in almost totally incomprehensible French, took him by the hand and led him upstairs to a salon where they exchanged polite banalities. Then, leaving Ferdinand to settle down, the Emperor rode back to the citadel to continue his manoeuvres.

His Grand Marshal informed Ferdinand on the Emperor's behalf that he was expected at Marrac that afternoon at four o'clock.

A superb carriage driven by a coachman in a tricorne hat and plumes was sent for the Prince and his entourage a few minutes before the appointed time.

The ensuing meeting was icily formal and the Emperor was

careful to avoid addressing Ferdinand by the titles of either
'Highness' or 'Majesty'; at his departure, he accompanied him
only to the door of the salon, thus observing the protocol of
a King towards a King's son.

As Canon Escoiquiz passed him with a low bow, the
Emperor suddenly advanced and seized him by the arm.
'Canon,' he said affably, 'I should like to have a few words
with you. Will you step this way? You will be driven back to
the Hotel Dubrocq a little later.'

The Canon was dumbfounded and also deeply flattered.
Napoleon had chosen to speak to *him* rather than to the
dukes and counts of the Prince's suite about the important
affairs which had brought them to Bayonne! Such an
honour . . .

Still smiling, the Emperor led the Canon back into the
salon, softly closed the door, and motioned him to take a
seat while he, following his custom, paced up and down with
his hands behind his back. The Canon reported the interview
in detail in his memoirs.

'Canon,' began the Emperor, 'I have been wanting to talk
to you about your Prince's affairs for a long time, all the
more so because I cannot but sympathize with his unfortunate father who has begged me to protect him. I cannot
refuse. The whole of Europe is watching me closely. The
circumstances in which Charles IV abdicated at Aranjuez,
surrounded as he was by seditious guards and a people in
revolt, point to his having been forced into taking this action;
as, at that time, my army was in Spain and indeed very close
to the court, it could be thought that I was partly to blame
for the uprising. This suspicion must be allayed; my honour
compels me to prove that I am incapable of such an unjust
and scandalous coup. I therefore cannot recognize Ferdinand
until his father, who has sent me a formal letter of protest
against his so-called renunciation, has freely re-enacted his
act of abdication in favour of his son.

'I shall be frank with you, Canon. The interests of my
empire require that the House of Bourbon, which is the

implacable enemy of my own, should be expelled from the
throne of Spain. This is also in the interest of your own
country which would enjoy a better constitution under my
dynasty. Charles IV is well aware that his children are
incapable of governing and, wishing to preserve his people
from the misfortunes that threaten them, is disposed to cede
his rights to me.

'However, since I esteem Ferdinand, who has shown his
trust in me by coming to Bayonne, I wish to compensate him
to a certain degree for what my policy requires him to give
up. You will therefore suggest to Ferdinand on my behalf
that in return for his renunciation of the Spanish throne I
shall give him that of Etruria with the title of King, and a
year's revenue in advance to enable him to establish himself
there. As soon as the treaty is signed, I shall give him my
niece in marriage — this as a further proof of friendship. If he
refuses to comply with my demands then I shall have to
reach an agreement with his father.'

The Canon swallowed hard; making an effort to conceal
his anger, he asked the Emperor whether he could speak to
him candidly.

'By all means, Canon, you are at liberty to say whatever
you like.'

'Then, sire, I will not conceal from you with what
astonishment I have listened to your proposal, which my
King and country never even suspected ...' He went on at
length to remind the Emperor of all that Spain had done to
support France, and of the sacrifices she had made: ships,
money, the free passage of French troops through the
country; he stressed Ferdinand's friendly disposition towards
him, his desire to marry a French princess which was put
forward at a time when such a project was considered
treasonable and he was imprisoned in the Escorial. Then he
proceeded to give a detailed account of the events which had
led up to the Aranjuez uprising, including a list of Godoy's
evil intentions and plan to oust the Prince in the event of
Charles's death.

'I am fully aware of all that,' Napoleon replied, 'but I repeat that the King's abdication was made under duress; the proof is that he protested as soon as he was free to do so — that is, the day after his abdication.'

The Canon launched into a further lengthy discourse. When he had finished, Napoleon smiled and, tweaking him by the ear, murmured: 'Let us leave all that on one side for the moment. Now tell me, Canon, frankly: how am I to blind myself to the fact that the interests of my dynasty and empire demand that the Bourbons should no longer rule in Spain? Even if all you have said were true, my answer would still have to be: bad policy!'

Escoiquiz replied heatedly that he had a closer acquaintance than Napoleon with the nature and spirit of the Spanish people, that it would be good policy and in Napoleon's interests to leave the Bourbons in Spain. Napoleon shook his head.

'How can I do better,' he replied, 'to justify my opinion in your eyes, than to remind you of the period in which King Charles himself, despite his pretence of fidelity to our alliance, determined to make war on me shortly before the battle of Jena, that is to say at the very moment when he believed me to be engaged in a war on Prussia? Did he not take advantage of the danger which threatened me to publish throughout the kingdom a proclamation whose object was nothing less than to arm his subjects against me? No, I shall never be able to rely upon Spain while the Bourbons are on the throne. Do not be surprised, Canon, if I repeat: it would be bad policy!'

Escoiquiz argued that the 1806 manifesto was the work of Godoy. He put up an excellent case for his royal master and stressed that if he were to be removed from the throne the Spaniards would vow the Emperor an implacable hatred and that other European countries would rise against him.

'You exaggerate, Canon,' the Emperor replied patiently, 'I do not fear the only European nation which could cause me some disquiet. The Emperor of Russia, to whom I communi-

cated my ideas about Spain at Tilsit, approved of them and
gave me his word that he would do nothing to oppose them.
The other powers would not move. The resistance of the
Spaniards would not be very serious. The rich, afraid of
losing their fortunes, will not raise a finger; the clergy and
monks, whom I would render responsible for any disorders,
would bring their influence to bear . . . believe me, Canon,
countries where there are many monks are easy to subjugate.
I know that from experience!'

The Canon retorted indignantly that knowing his countrymen as he did he could predict that the rich, the clergy and
the monks would in fact be the first to set the example of
resistance and self-sacrifice to the nation and that the entire
populace would be opposed to the elevation of a foreign king
to the throne of Spain.

'Even if that were so,' the Emperor replied calmly, 'I
would win in the long run. I am prepared to sacrifice 200,000
men but I am far from believing that I would require that
many to conquer Spain.'

'If, after a bloody war, the Spaniards *were* conquered,'
exclaimed the Canon, 'do you think that the new French
dynasty would sit at ease on the throne? Sooner or later they
would find that they were sitting on a volcano that would
explode under their feet. England, envious of France, would
help the conquered slaves to rise. The war in Spain would
turn into an indestructible hydra. What good would a ruined
Spain be to France?'

'Really, Canon, you go too far. Those dire predictions are,
if I may say so, mere castles in Spain,' said the Emperor,
laughing tolerantly.

The Canon alluded once more to Ferdinand's proposed
marriage with a French princess. This, he said, would be a
guarantee of permanent friendly relations between the two
countries, provided that Ferdinand remained on the throne
of Spain. Napoleon looked sceptical, as well he might, since
he had no princess to offer.

'An alliance through a woman is too weak a link to fix the

political conduct of a prince. It is not comparable to the links between relatives of the same stock. Who can be sure that a French princess would have any influence upon Ferdinand? So many circumstances can alter the situation. Death too can sever links. Young as he is, can you guarantee that Ferdinand will have the same confidence in you six months from now. The first able courtier will be able to cheat him and obtain his favour. Do you really believe I would have the same security with the Bourbons on the throne as if the sceptre were in the hands of a prince of my own family? He may have disagreements with me but never to the point of being my declared enemy.'

'If we had known what was in your mind, we would not have crossed the Bidassoa,' said the Canon bitterly.

Napoleon wheeled round and asked him with interest: 'What measures would you have taken if you had not come to Bayonne?'

'I would have arranged for King Ferdinand to escape.'

'Where to?'

'Algeciras, near Gibraltar.'

'And then?'

'If Your Imperial Majesty had refused to leave Spain we would have waged war till the bitter end.'

'You were right. That would have been the best thing to do.'

'Ah, if only that perfidious Prince of the Peace had not constantly thwarted us,' the Canon began, but Napoleon interrupted him.

'That is not just. He has not been such a bad politician as you make out.'

Indeed, Canon Escoiquiz's plan to move Ferdinand to the south of Spain, which had been mooted in Madrid for a short while, was similar to Godoy's foiled attempt to remove The Kings to Andalusia. Only the antagonisms between the Prince and the favourite had placed them and Spain in the Emperor's grasp.

Once again Napoleon playfully tweaked the Canon's ear. 'I

am really sorry, Canon,' he told him, 'that you absolutely refuse to share my views.'

'I wish, sire, that I could persuade Your Imperial Majesty to share mine, even though it were to cost me my ears,' the Canon replied ruefully, as he rubbed the one that Napoleon had just tweaked rather too hard.

He was driven back to the Hotel Dubrocq in a daze. There he found Ferdinand hunched in an armchair on the first floor, sunk in despair.

'You do not have to tell me what has happened,' he said before the Canon opened his mouth. 'I know. General Savary has been here to deliver the Emperor's verdict. He offers me the kingdom of Etruria and his niece's hand. A mere pretext. It's despicable. I must have some air . . . ' He rose and walked over to the window, opened it and stepped on to the balcony. A cool breeze swept in from the Atlantic.

A crowd of about a hundred people had gathered below; among them were the captains of some Spanish fishing vessels anchored in the port of Bayonne.

'*Viva Fernando*!' they shouted fervently.

Ferdinand pulled a handkerchief from his pocket and waved back. 'I have been betrayed!' he cried.

'Then let us carry you off in one of our boats!' shouted one of the loyal Spaniards.

There was a movement in the crowd as a group of French officers advanced to disperse them. A guard disguised as a valet suddenly appeared behind Ferdinand. 'It is getting chilly, Your Highness, would it not be better for you to go inside?' he suggested blandly, advancing quickly to close the shutters.

It was too late to escape. The trap had well and truly closed.

XXXV

In Madrid, Charles and Maria Luisa continued to plead for the release of Godoy who had been transferred to the castle of Villaviciosa nearer the capital. Never once did the sovereigns refer to their personal safety or future; their only concern was for their beloved Manuel.

'Is the Grand Duke aware,' wrote the Queen shortly after Ferdinand's departure for Bayonne,

that they have begun to cross-examine the Prince of the Peace? It is clear that they intend to have a trial and to rush it through so that they can execute him before the Emperor has set him free. Your Highness will not suffer your friend to perish – you *will* free him from his terrible predicament and God grant that what they have already done to him does not cause his death! We ask this for him as much as for ourselves – nay, more than ourselves. Grant to the King and me this favour, the only favour of importance we ask from you.

Charles sent the Grand Duke the present of a horse which, wrote the Queen,

will serve you well even if it is rather old. The horse is called Farnesio and is dark chestnut. It has a slight growth in one ear and is rising fifteen. It should be good for another four of five years' service. It is a splendid war horse and is the best trotter and galloper going. At the moment it is a little bit lame owing to the faulty treatment of a damaged hoof. But that is a trifle. Farnesio is absolutely the best horse the King has; that is why he is presenting it with his compliments to the Grand Duke of Berg.

The only way to save Godoy was to put pressure on the Council of Castile. The Grand Duke of Berg advised Charles to write to the President, his brother the Infante Don Antonio, and he promised his support. Charles wrote on 17 April, stressing boldly that his abdication had been forced upon him, that it was null and void and that he was under the protection of his ally, the Emperor Napoleon, whom he was preparing to go and meet.

On 21 April the Grand Duke summoned the council to

issue orders for the release of Godoy. They complied
cravenly and sent orders to his keeper, the Marquis of
Castelar, who handed over his prisoner to General Exelmans
and Colonel Rosetti on behalf of the Grand Duke of Berg.
The Spanish leaders were capitulating on every front.

The Prince of the Peace, wearing slippers and a military
coat over his torn uniform, scrambled hastily into the waiting
carriage and cowered on the floor for fear of being
recognized. He was driven first to the French camp at
Chamartin and then escorted to Bayonne in accordance with
Napoleon's orders.

'The Emperor does not know the Spanish,' observed
Remond, a police officer attached to Murat. 'They will never
forgive him for having snatched their prey from them.'

The letter in which the Infante Don Antonio reported
Godoy's release to Ferdinand in Bayonne was characteristic
of the way in which the various members of the Spanish
royal family referred to each other in their intimate and even
public correspondence:

The vermin Maria Luisa writes gleefully to the Grand Duke of Berg
and has obtained from him the release of the sausage-selling Prince, but
it is your ineffable father who begged more warmly still that the
sausage-seller might be freed and not have his head cut off. The tender
pair are still at the Escorial, guarded by those traitors of French
carabiniers and the soldiers under General Wattier, a drunkard who
snores at table when the dessert is brought; this I have from a good
source . . .

Your father, who is crippled with rheumatism, says that his aches are
thorns which you have nailed into his heart. Where the devil did my
brother pick up such elegant expressions? The vermin must have put
them into his head. Murat pretended that it was you, when you were
just setting out from Madrid, who gave orders for Godoy's release. What
rubbish! My colleagues gave way like the poor fish they are, so you will
soon be seeing the favourite again. Why was he not hanged as I advised
you to? Luisetta of Etruria asserts that she talked about it with Murat
in his bedroom. Was ever a woman so unblushing?

It had been rumoured for some time that Luisetta had had
a flirtation with Murat which began when they first met in
Florence.

In Ferdinand's unguarded reply to his uncle dated 28 April he warned him that

Napoleon has a letter from my parents in his hands saying that father's abdication was forced upon him. Act as though you didn't know but behave in consequence and try not to be influenced by those cursed Frenchmen.

The word *'maldito'*, translated by 'cursed' in Spanish, does not have such a strong implication in that language, but Napoleon, who had the letter intercepted and translated, was incensed by the Prince's use of the word. It confirmed his opinion that Ferdinand was 'both wicked and stupid'. All his mail to Madrid was intercepted and taken to the Emperor.

As the mice were driven one by one into his trap, Napoleon described them in a series of letters to Monsieur de Talleyrand, Prince of Benevento. Author, producer and director of the drama which was drawing to its close ('the fifth act is about to begin,' he wrote to Talleyrand), he was curious about the characters whom until then he had manipulated from a distance but never actually seen.

The Prince of Asturias is a brute, a bad lot [he stressed over and over again] and an enemy of France. You can imagine that with my experience of managing men, his twenty-four years quite failed to impress me; indeed, my mind is so clear about him that nothing would induce me to recognize him as King of Spain. Further than that, I notified him that as King Charles was on the French frontier I could not have any more dealings with him. As a consequence of this decision, I have arrested his messengers and found on them letters full of venomous hatred against the French whom he repeatedly described as 'these damned Frenchmen'.

In another letter, the Emperor added:

The Prince is so stupid that he hardly ever speaks. He never answers to what one says to him. Reproach him, tease him, he never changes countenance. His character can be summed up in one word: crafty. He is also very materialistic; he does nothing but eat four times a day.

This opinion was not very different from that of the Prince's own mother who became exasperated when her son refused to answer her.

Napoleon's attitude towards Ferdinand hardened appreciably when he and his entourage, after much deliberation, firmly rejected the offer to exchange the crown of Spain for that of little Etruria, so soon to be taken over by France. It does not say much for Canon Escoiquiz's sagacity that he was one of the members of Ferdinand's council who voted in favour of the ignominious proposal in the belief that half a cake was better than none. Even after his interview with Napoleon and the latter's evident duplicity, he still retained traces of unbelievable naivety vis à vis the Emperor.

In the meantime, Godoy reached Bayonne on 26 April. Napoleon described him to Talleyrand as follows:

> He has the appearance of a bull with something of Daru thown in. He has been treated with barbarity but is beginning to pull himself together. It is as well that the untrue imputations against him have been withdrawn. It is important that he should be regarded with veiled contempt.

The Emperor had probably heard by then that the enormous riches attributed to the favourite were not as exorbitant as had been reported. Furthermore, as he had told Escoiquiz, he did not really believe that Godoy had been such a bad politician in the circumstances. He had repeatedly endeavoured to resist Napoleon's demands, in the interest of his Kings and country. As for his attempt to procure a little kingdom of his own in Portugal, that too was understandable in view of Ferdinand's attitude. There was little clemency to be expected from that quarter, as Maria Luisa had said.

'I must unravel this tangle within the next few days,' Napoleon wrote to Murat. The denouement was taking a little longer than he had anticipated and his entourage found him bad-tempered and curt. The arrival of Josephine from Bordeaux on 27 April soothed him a little, but what he missed most was the wise, conciliating presence of Monsieur de Talleyrand.

Josephine remonstrated with the Emperor, to his great annoyance. He did not like her to interfere in affairs of state. 'What does it matter to you,' he cried impatiently, 'whether Charles IV or Ferdinand treats with me?' He added under his breath: 'My political carriage has started; it must go on. Woe to him who finds himself beneath its wheels!'

Irritated by Josephine's worried silence, he went on: 'Do you think my policy is in accordance with the feelings of my heart? No, not at all, but there are sometimes extraordinary cases – and this is one of them – when I must suppress my personal feelings and devote myself to the good of my people and the glory which must necessarily be reflected upon my crown.' A crown with several branches; he had now heard that his brother Joseph was willing to accept that of Spain.

The Emperor was taking upon himself the mantle of Louis XIV who had placed one of his grandsons upon the throne of Spain and who had sent ministers to advise him, notably Choiseul. Napoleon believed in his megalomania that he was the equal of a king and his dynasty and that France could govern Spain more effectively than the Bourbons ever could. In that he was probably right, but nations are not governed by reason alone.

XXXVI

Charles and Maria Luisa reached Bayonne on 28 April. They had packed hastily; it had been difficult to decide how much luggage to bring with them. The Queen had had her diamonds – those that she had displayed with so much pride to Lady Holland five years before – placed in three caskets hidden inside the seats of her carriage. Before leaving San Lorenzo she had paid a last visit to the royal chapel to make a personal selection from the vast repository of holy relics: eleven bodies of saints, 103 skulls, 600 arms and legs, 1,400 fingers, bones and scalps, all with little cards tied on to them recording the supposed identity of their late owners. While the Queen deliberated on this issue Charles personally supervised the packing of his favourite clocks. A selection had to be made among them; he was sad to have to part with so many, but his choicest specimens accompanied him into exile in a special coach.

The Kings left Spain, to which they were never to return, without regrets. All they were concerned about was their personal safety, now that they knew Manuel was also on his way to France.

From Aranda del Duero, where his son had spent a night ten days before, Charles wrote effusively to Napoleon:

We shall find a balm to our wounded hearts under your protection. The Queen is writing to you too. I look forward to falling into your arms.

His son had used a similar expression. 'Falling into your arms!' How the Emperor must have smiled. The mice could not run quickly enough into the trap he had set for them!

Napoleon gave orders for The Kings to be received with the honours due to their rank. Troops lined the road leading into Bayonne, where the civil authorities assembled to greet them, salvoes were fired from the citadel and fortifications; the royal carriage was escorted by the nobles sent to welcome them at the frontier – the Duke of Plaisance, the Prince of Neuchâtel, Counts Reille, du Manoir, d'Audenarde. The Kings were treated more royally than they had been in their own country.

A great concourse of people awaited the monarch's arrival in Bayonne, for the Spanish sovereigns were believed to belong to an almost mythical realm and Bourbon princes in general to a bygone age. This impression was confirmed when the ancient carriages dating from the time of Louis XIV drew up before the house assigned for The Kings' residence, in the same street as the Hotel Dubrocq where their sons were staying.

It was observed with astonishment that Spanish royal etiquette, always so demanding, had been rigidly adhered to by the sovereigns; four unfortunate liveried postilions had been obliged to stand at the back of the royal carriage all the way from the Escorial to Bayonne, a distance of close on four hundred miles, come dust, come rain, come mountain sleet. Upon their arrival they were as stiff as Egyptian mummies and had to be practically lifted off the step and carried away on stretchers.

Even the King climbed out of his carriage with difficulty, but this was because of his gout. He looked round affably after he alighted, speaking to all and sundry with ease and simplicity. Everybody recognized his Bourbon features, the long nose and protruding chin. 'He could be French,' they remarked, seeing his likeness to his unfortunate cousin Louis XVI. They thought that the Queen looked Italian. Her sprightly vivacity made a good impression. On the surface she was charming.

Ferdinand and his brother the Infante Don Carlos had come to greet their parents and were waiting at the foot of the stairs, but as soon as the King caught sight of his heir he reddened and shouted angrily: 'Be off with you – have you not made me suffer enough?' Then he turned and stretched out his arms to Godoy who advanced to embrace him.

Ferdinand turned pale and stepped back. The Queen, perhaps to save appearances, embraced her two sons briefly, then burst into tears of joy when she set eyes on Godoy. The contrast in the reception of sons and favourite was all too apparent. The 'Trinity' retired to their apartments before receiving the Spanish grandees who had come to attend the hand-kissing ceremony demanded by Spanish protocol, and the scorned Infantes returned to the Hotel Dubrocq.

Soon after The Kings' arrival Napoleon came to greet them personally and invite them to dine with him at the Château de Marrac on the following day, after they had had time to rest from their fatiguing journey.

King Charles is a fine fellow [he wrote to Talleyrand soon after he had set eyes on him]. I don't know whether it is because of his position or his circumstances, but he has the air of an honest and good-natured man. The Queen wears her history and infatuation on her face. It is terrifying. There is no need for me to say more. It surpasses all that one can imagine. They are both dining with me today . . .

The dinner was preceded by a visit to the Empress Josephine, who received the sovereigns with her customary grace and savoir faire. Napoleon had invited her to Bayonne for that express purpose – to cover his political ambush under a display of charm and social polish. Josephine was the perfect hostess. The mice were to be given a party before the trapdoor finally closed upon them.

Maria Luisa and Josephine discussed toilettes and hair-styles and the Empress promised to send the Queen her valet-coiffeur Duplan to teach her maids how to arrange her hair in the latest fashion. Duplan did his best with the Queen's hair but, in the words of one of the dinner guests, 'Duplan's exertions were in vain. All his great talent could not make the Queen look beautiful. She just looked different, that's all.'

Charles had difficulty in climbing into the new-fangled French coach sent for him and Maria Luisa that evening; his sword, too, got in his way, but he was the first to laugh good-humouredly at these little mishaps.

When he got out in front of the Château doorway, Napoleon advanced to help him up the steps. Charles murmured sadly: 'It's because I am so infirm that they wanted to get rid of me.'

The Emperor replied jovially: 'We shall see about that. Lean on me; I have enough strength for two.'

'That is what I believe and hope,' the King said. It was a spectacle worthy of Goya's acid brush: the weak, crippled King tottering up the steps on the arm of his cynical, all-powerful enemy with whom he was about to dine.

Then the Emperor lent his arm to Maria Luisa and led her at a brisk martial pace into the dining-room. Turning suddenly, he halted and exclaimed: 'Pray forgive me, Madam, am I walking too fast?' Maria Luisa smiled archly as she replied: 'I understand that that is your habit, sire.'

The Emperor was relieved that Josephine was present to help endure the banalities of table conversation at which she was so adept. Maria Luisa, not to be outdone, spoke amusingly about court etiquette in Spain, but her Italian-Hispano-French accent was difficult to follow.

Charles, now perfectly relaxed, ate with gusto and app-reciated the French cuisine. 'Have some more goose pâté,' he urged Maria Luisa, 'it is really excellent.'

In answer to a question put to him by Josephine about the kind of life he led in his different palaces, the King innocently replied: 'I used to hunt every day. In the evening, Manuel would tell me whether things were going well or ill and then I went to bed.' He was really quite senile. His French hosts exchanged bewildered glances and the Emperor passed a napkin across his mouth to conceal a derisive smile.

XXXVII

There were to be no more parties after that evening. The next day negotiations began in earnest.

Ferdinand was summoned to confront his father and the following extraordinary conversation, recorded by Canon Escoiquiz in his memoirs, took place between them, after the King had declared that he wanted his son to give him back his crown.

'Dear father,' Ferdinand expostulated, 'if you did not renounce the crown at Aranjuez of your own volition, why did you not tell me so then, knowing full well that if such had been the case, I would never have accepted it?'

'I renounced it voluntarily,' Charles replied petulantly.

'Then why have you gone back on your decision?'

'Because it was never my intention that the renunciation should be permanent, but only temporary.'

'Then why did you not include a clause to that effect in your act of abdication? Or tell me in private of your real intentions?'

'Because I did not feel like doing so and I was under no obligation to tell you.'

'Was Your Majesty in any way forced to make your renunciation?'

'No, I made it myself because I wanted to; nobody forced me.'

'And you now wish to reign once more?'

'No, I am very far from wishing to do that.'

'Then why do you order me to give you back the crown?'

'Because I want to. I do not have to tell you the reason why; nor do I wish you to utter another word on the subject. I only want you to obey me.'

The senile King had obviously been prompted by Napoleon and spurred by Maria Luisa, who preferred anyone except her own son to reign over Spain. Both she and Godoy knew that in the event of their joint retirement in France they would be granted an adequate pension by the Emperor, whereas Ferdinand would give them nothing. That was all that the 'Trinity' now aspired to: an old age pension in a French palace, free from duties and responsibilities. Charles's dignity, the royal pose he adopted for portraits and official functions, was a pitiful façade, a masquerade. Never strong-willed, undermined by a succession of illnesses and attacks, he was now reduced to the state of a helpless puppet.

Godoy, after his recent experiences in prison, had no desire to return to a country which had no use for him and which would have exulted in his execution. He wanted only one favour from the Emperor, and that was granted to him: the presence of Pepita Tudó and of his children Carlota and Luis. They were called to Bayonne to join their respective lover and father. Maria Luisa must have been deeply attached to Godoy, with a love compounded of passion and maternal solicitude, to accede to her favourite's demand. When Napoleon said that 'her history is written upon her face', he was being hasty and unfair, swayed by the tittle-tattle he had heard about the Queen and by his own Corsican standard of double morality. To this one must add his veneration of his extremely austere and moral mother.

The Queen's *character* certainly showed in her face and

Ferdinand's was very similar. Both revealed craftiness, cruelty, vindictiveness, but not the passions of their private life. Until then, as far as Ferdinand was concerned, his life had been obligatorily chaste. He would make up for it later on in his life.

After his meeting with his father, Ferdinand went back to confer with his council; together they drafted a letter, a model of dignity and sobriety, which was handed to the King on 1 May.

In this letter the Prince stressed that the King's abdication at Aranjuez had been voluntary as the King himself had declared in their conversation at Bayonne the day before.

When I asked you whether you wanted to return to the throne you replied that you neither desired to reign nor return to Spain. In spite of this statement you ordered me to give up the crown.

The Prince declared that he was willing to make this renunciation on condition that the King returned to Madrid and made his abdication before the assembled Cortes. His Majesty, however, should not be accompanied by 'persons who are justly hated by the nation' meaning, of course, Godoy. If His Majesty was opposed to this procedure the Prince suggested that he would govern in his name as his lieutenant. (It will be remembered that he had made a similar suggestion before the uprising of Aranjuez.)

These terms were sensible and legitimate, but they confused the King and irritated Napoleon who dictated a long reply to which the King appended his signature on 2 May. In this document the King put all the blame for the current situation and chaos in Spain on Ferdinand's shoulders (and on those of his poor little late wife) and wrote that he placed himself entirely in the hands of Napoleon 'who has shown me your letters which prove how much you hate France . . . and he has declared that he would never recognize you as King'. Charles concluded, ominously, that he would 'go to his grave and pardon his son for all the bitterness of his last years after he had assured himself that the religion of Spain would be maintained together with the integrity and independence of its provinces'. This was the prelude to the treaty which the Emperor had already drafted in his mind if not yet on paper.

The Prince replied point by point to this letter on 4 May, refuting the King's fallacious and hypocritical arguments (dictated by Napoleon) and referring to his letter addressed to Napoleon at Vitoria. Ferdinand reiterated that he had proved his desire to maintain good relations with France by writing to the Emperor immediately after his father's abdication and by expressing his wish to marry a French princess, as he had already done before. In conclusion he stated that he, Ferdinand, and none other, was legally empowered to represent the King in the event of his refusing to reign.

The present state of affairs has been provoked with the sole intention of eliminating our family from the throne of Spain forever and of replacing it by a member of the French imperial family. This cannot be effected without the consent of the Spanish nation through its representatives, and not on foreign soil.

The Emperor was in a dilemma. What could he do to force Ferdinand to cede his rights? Charles, abetted by Maria Luisa and Godoy, had been easy to manipulate; Ferdinand and his advisers were being more obstinate and courageous than he had anticipated. But, knowing that Ferdinand, if dealt with alone, could be easily frightened — he had said as much to Talleyrand in one of his letters — Napoleon asked Charles to call his son for a further meeting.

On this occasion Napoleon was present, frowning and awe-inspiring.

As soon as Ferdinand entered the room the King exploded with wrath and demanded the restoration of his crown. Napoleon interjected forcefully that he was bound to protect an unfortunate King and father against a rebellious son who had wounded him most cruelly. When the Prince opened his mouth to speak the King ordered him to be silent and he began to hurl violent accusations against him, even threatening him with his stick.

Accustomed though he was to dramatic scenes, which he often provoked himself, Napoleon was shattered by this outburst of paternal hatred. Upon his return to the Château de Marrac he summoned Josephine and his personal entourage, including the Abbé de Pradt, one of the Bayonne negotiators, and described the confrontation in which he had just taken part with a mimicry and dramatic power — wrote the Abbé in his memoirs — of which nobody had until then believed him capable. Pacing up and down the garden he re-enacted the interview which, he said, reminded him of certain passages of Corneille's tragedies.

'Charles accused his son of conspiring against him, of outraging his white hair . . . he was like the King of Priam. The scene was becoming more and more impressive when the Queen burst in and interrupted it with a wealth of threats and invectives. After reproaching her son for having dethroned his parents she asked me — yes, me — to send him to the scaffold. What a woman! What a mother! She horrified me. I felt sorry for the Prince at that moment.'

After a short silence, the Emperor added unexpectedly: 'There is only one man with any imagination in that lot: the Prince of the Peace. He wanted The Kings to go to South America. That would have been splendid and no doubt he would have brought it off if the Aranjuez uprising had not occurred.'

The Emperor then digressed, in poetic vein, upon the grandeur of the thrones of Mexico and Peru, the sovereigns who would take possession of them, and the effects which they could have upon the entire world.

The Emperor was sublime [wrote the Abbé Pradt]. I had never heard him speak in such imaginative turns of phrase. He was carried away. Was it because the theme inspired him and that his faculties had been stimulated by the scene which he had just witnessed? His eloquence attained heights which he has never since surpassed.

Napoleon had no doubt expressed in words, swept by his Mediterranean imagination, the stuff of which his imperial dreams were made: far away lands full of still unexploited treasures, golden thrones and powerful sovereigns extending their sway over vast territories, violent clashes of personalities, colourful speeches, heroic roles, grand opera.

It should however be stated for the record that Napoleon's outburst strangely resembled the terms in which the French ambassador in Florence, Count Hector d'Aubusson de la Feuillarde, had written to the Minister for Foreign Affairs, Monsieur de Talleyrand, on 26 December 1806, and which Count Sixte de Bourbon refers to in his book on the Queen of Etruria, Luisetta. After having stated that in his opinion the Bourbons would always be the adversaries of France, the Count observed:

The only way to calm all the agitation would be to remove the Bourbons and replace them by members of the imperial family. The New World would then become a compensation of great advantage to them. The King of Spain could be established in Mexico, the Queen of Etruria in Cuba. The French could obtain the privilege of being the only people allowed to cross the canal which could be cut through to the Pacific by the lake of Nicaragua, an easy feat which would enhance trade and constitute a new passage to attack the English in India. It is time that the old reigning families of Europe should give way to a hero to whom Europe owes its regeneration . . . they have had their faculties both moral and mental destroyed and weakened by their very antiquity . . .

Talleyrand must have communicated this report to the Emperor and there is no doubt that it fired his imagination.

While Napoleon was ruminating upon his next move, events once more played into his hands.

On the afternoon of 5 May, when he was taking his afternoon ride in the company of General Savary, a breathless estafette, Monsieur Danencourt, galloped up to him with an urgent dispatch from Murat giving the details of an uprising which had taken place in Madrid on 2 May.

This was the answer to Napoleon's problem, the weapon which would crush Ferdinand's resistance, the last obstacle to his plan for the usurpation of the Spanish throne. He turned

his horse and hurried to the King's residence, assuming
– General Savary wrote in his memoirs – the ferocious
expression that had so often reduced his staff and subordin-
ates to a state of abject terror.

XXXVIII

What had happened in Madrid?

As the days went by without any news from Bayonne,
where it was known that the royal family and Godoy had
been summoned by the Emperor, the masses began to grow
restless and resentful. One of Murat's aides-de-camp was
assaulted in broad daylight; a Madrilenian attacked a French
officer escorted by two soldiers; more incidents followed and
news filtered in almost daily of similar attacks upon the
French in the provinces. Murat began to be seriously alarmed.

An eye-witness account of the events of 2 and 3 May,
immortalized by Goya's paintings, was found by the historian
Pérez de Guzmán in the Spanish royal archives of Madrid
fifty years ago. It was written by José Molina, a member of
the royal household. This is how he described the events of
the day that triggered off the Peninsular War.

At 8.30 a.m. two carriages drove quietly up to the royal
palace from where the heavily-veiled ex-Queen of Etruria
emerged with her servants. She climbed quickly into the
carriage and it made off up the Calle del Tesoro. The second
carriage was stationed at the Puerta del Principe of the
palace.

A man detached himself from the crowd that had taken to
strolling past the palace daily to find out what, if anything,
was happening, walked boldly up to the gates and demanded
to know who the coach was waiting for. The coachman
replied: 'The Infante Don Francisco de Paula.' The unknown
man then pushed his way past the sentries at the door and
asked the servants inside whether this was correct. He rushed

out, when they had confirmed that it was so, shouting:
'Treason! Treason! They have taken the King from us, now
they want to take the rest of the royal family. Death to the
French — we must not let the Infante go!'

The crowd took up the cry and began to push forward. A
window on the first floor was opened and a figure appeared.
Molina called him 'a grandee' but he may simply have been
one of the palace upper servants; he began to harangue the
crowd: 'Citizens — to arms — they are taking away the
Infante!'

From sixty to seventy people stormed the palace, climbed
up the stairs, reached the galleries on the first floor and ran
towards the Infante's apartments, guided by the servants. The
door was blocked by the chief of the royal guards, Don Pedro
de Torres. '*Por Dios*, be calm!' he exhorted the advancing
horde, 'we have enough people to protect us as it is.'

'By Christ,' replied the leader of the insurgents, 'we
Madrilenians don't need anybody to tell us what to do.' The
door behind Don Pedro opened to reveal the fourteen-
year-old Infante Francisco; he was pale and trembling with
emotion and excitement. As soon as the people saw him they
fell upon their knees; those in front stooped to kiss his little
hands. 'Long live the Infante, we shall defend him to the
death,' they cried passionately.

The Infante made an all-embracing gesture and offered to
show himself to the people from the balcony. When he
stepped out and blew kisses to the crowds below they
imagined they saw tears in his eyes and another shout went
up: 'It's the Infante Don Francisco! He does not want to
leave — see, he is crying — they are going to kidnap him!'

At this the crowd hurled themselves at the waiting coach.
The horses reared and were unharnessed from their traces.
Murat, who had been informed of what was going on — he
had in any case heard the shouts since his residence was only
a hundred yards or so away from the palace — sent a couple
of officers, La Grange and Compiègne, to find out what was
happening. They rode up, brandishing their swords with

threatening gestures, and were greeted by cries of: 'Kill them; don't let any Frenchman enter the palace precincts!' The officers pointed their swords at the mob who surrounded them but the Walloon guards galloped up just in time to placate them and save the officers' lives. A few minutes later Murat's personal guards escorted the officers back to his palace.

O'Farill, the Minister for War, rushed out of the royal palace and, catching sight of Molina, snapped: 'Get these rebels back to their homes – we don't need them!'

The crowd began to pick up stones and sticks to throw at the French soldiers sent by Murat to restore order. A small determined band of men forced their way into the royal armoury from where they emerged with the sword alleged to have belonged to the national hero, El Cid. They had thus avenged the loss of Francis I's sword carried off by Murat. The sword of El Cid was a symbol of Spanish nationhood and they took it in their hands and held it aloft with a clumsy gesture of rough reverence. 'Long live Ferdinand!' they cried hoarsely, the light of battle in their eyes.

One battalion and two cannons were rushed over to clear the space in front of the palace. A general alarm was sounded. A regiment was sent from the Retiro where General Grouchy was wounded by the insurgents. A band of fusiliers preceded by turbaned Mamelouks galloped up the narrow Calle de la Platería, cuirassiers dashed up the Calle de Toledo, others advanced from the Calle de Fuencarral, converging upon the city's centre, the Puerta del Sol, accompanied by the sounds of stampeding horses, the crackle of musket fire and menacing cries uttered in French, Polish, German and Arabic by the soldiers recruited from every land which Napoleon had conquered.

Don Antonio and the members of the council were scared out of their feeble wits by an insurrection which could easily be the beginning of a civil war. They cravenly relied upon Murat's troops to disperse the motley crowd of rebels composed of beggars, peasants, artisans, shopkeepers and

members of the liberal classes. The *manolas* of the Barrio del
Barquillo hurled bricks and tiles from the rooftops; one of
them killed the son of General Legrand. A priest joined the
insurgents in the Barrio de San Isidro; an architect, Alfonso
Sanchez, directed the men and women of the Barrio de
Toledo; a coal-merchant, César Mora, distributed pistols, and
a hotel proprietor, José Albarrada, in the Calle de San
Bernardo, joined in the fray and joined the crowd on its way
to the barracks at the end of the street, occupied by a mixed
detachment of French and Spanish troops; the gates were
hurriedly closed against them and they were left standing
outside, hurling abuse at the occupants.

A Spanish artillery captain, Pedro Velarde, advanced and
implored his countrymen to open the door. The senior
Spanish officer, Louis Daoiz, was a friend of Velarde. He
hesitated for a moment, then – hearing the cry of 'Long live
the artillery, long live the King!' – he shouted: 'Open the
doors – open the gates,' and the excited mob poured in to
seize all the muskets and ammunition they could lay their
hands on.

As a detachment of troops from the Westphalian battalion
advanced up the narrow street the five cannons in the yard
were hurriedly placed in position. The small band of
Spaniards opened fire. Men and women manned the guns
while the artillerymen hastily manufactured cartridges. Clara
del Rey, Manuela Malesa, Maria Beano, were three of the
women who died as they threw themselves in front of the
advancing troops captained by General Lagrange.

At first the French, finding it difficult to manoeuvre in the
narrow street, were mown down, but they were soon
reinforced and gained the upper hand. A cannon ball cut off
Daoiz's right leg; he leaned on a rifle and continued to give
orders until General Lagrange walked over the corpses and
ran him through with his sword. Another cannon ball killed
his friend Velarde. In forty-five minutes the battle ended
through lack of ammunition and – almost – of combatants.
The smoke-filled street emptied. Only corpses remained in

pools of blood.

It was now two o'clock in the afternoon. A patrol of French and Spanish officers and councillors from the Junta rode down the Calle de Alcalá waving white handkerchiefs and shouting: 'Citizens! All is over. Go back to your homes. Peace has been restored.'

Murat published a decree exhorting people to be calm.

Charles IV is in Bayonne with his son. They have placed themselves under the protection of our Emperor who will be their arbiter. You must have complete confidence in His Imperial Majesty.

Before Government House in the Puerta del Sol a knot of men discussed the morning's events in hushed tones. One of them was overheard to say: 'The Grand Duke has convened a military commission. There's going to be a bloody repression.'

He was right. To General Lagrange's request for orders concerning the imprisoned rebel leaders, Murat curtly replied: 'General, I only want to know one thing: that the rebels have been exterminated.' He issued a further decree: 'Every village in which a Frenchman is killed will be burned. Those found to be in possession of arms will be shot.' He took over the presidency of the Junta 'until the quarrels within the royal family have been resolved'.

The cold-blooded shooting of the rebel leaders took place in the Prado and the Monte Pio. Goya has immortalized the scene: the wild-eyed men in white shirts, arms raised in a final gesture of defiance; a few feet away from them the firing squad of carabiniers in their tall fur hats and black boots, poised squarely with rifles raised. What Napoleon's most perceptive advisers had feared and warned him against had happened at last: the Spaniards' indomitable patriotism had been aroused. From then on there would be no holding them back.

XXXIX

Nevertheless, Murat's dispatch to Napoleon gave a highly exaggerated figure of several thousand casualties in the 2 May uprising. A later estimate of under one thousand was nearer the truth, but the first figure suited the Emperor's purpose better.

He strode into Charles's apartments and tossed the dispatch to him, shouting angrily: 'See what I have just received from Madrid!'

Charles blanched and turned to Godoy: 'Manuel, send for Ferdinand and Carlos.' To Napoleon he said: 'I am much deceived if those villains have not had something to do with this business. I am shocked and horrified, but nothing can surprise me any more.'

When Ferdinand was shown in the King asked him sternly: 'Have you had any news from Madrid? Well, I can give you some', and he handed him Murat's dispatch.

'I know nothing about this, father, nothing,' stammered the Prince, standing before the impromptu tribunal composed of the King, the Queen, Godoy and Napoleon.

'Do you wish me to believe,' cried the King, 'that you have had nothing to do with this ... you or the wretches who govern you? Was it for the purpose of having my subjects massacred that you were in such a hurry to chase me from the throne? Tell me, do you expect to reign long by such means? Who has advised you? Do you want to gain the reputation of an assassin? Speak – speak – say something!'

But Ferdinand, overcome by humiliation, certain that he was facing a wall of deliberate incomprehension, remained speechless, as he had so often done in the past. He had shrunk to the size and mentality of a bullied schoolboy.

'How often did I warn you that you would bring disgrace upon yourself,' screamed Maria Luisa. 'See what you have come to, and brought us to! You would have had us massacred too if we had stayed in Madrid. How could you have prevented it?' She added, 'Speak ... that's how you have always behaved. For every new folly you commit you have nothing to say, nothing!' The Queen raised her hand as if to strike him and the King raised his stick. Ferdinand backed.

Napoleon dealt the final thrust. 'Prince, until now I had not made up my mind about the events which have brought you here, but the blood shed at Madrid has forced me to take a decision. The massacre can only be the work of a party which you cannot disavow, and I shall never recognize as King of Spain one who has broken the alliance which has so long united that country to France by provoking the assassination of French soldiers at the very moment he was asking me to sanction the impious act by which he wished to ascend the throne. You have been misled by bad advisers. I have obligations only towards the King your father; it is he whom I recognize and I shall have him escorted back to Madrid if he so desires.'

'I don't want to go back,' Charles declared flatly. 'What would I do in a country where passions have been let loose against me by my son? I would find rebellious subjects everywhere. After having had the happiness of a peaceful reign while the whole of Europe was torn by wars and conflicts, am I going to dishonour my old age by waging war on the provinces I have had the joy to preserve, and lead my subjects to the scaffold? No, I do not wish to do this. My son will accomplish the task better than I can. I wish to have nothing to do with it.'

Maria Luisa burst into a torrent of abuse against her son; under the violence of her language, the piercing shrillness of that dreaded voice which had haunted him since his childhood, the severity of his father and Napoleon's implacability, Ferdinand crumpled.

Seeing that he was broken beyond endurance, the Emperor seized his chance and pronounced the fatal words: 'Prince, you must choose between submission and the death of a rebel! You have until tomorrow morning to give the crown back to your father.'

Trembling with fear, Ferdinand capitulated. He was ready to sign anything. What else could he and his feeble party do against such odds?

'Only an inherently wicked person could have resorted to poisoning the old age of such a venerable father,' Napoleon exclaimed after Ferdinand had gone. He stayed behind with The Kings for a quarter of an hour and, after asking Godoy to join him later at the Château de Marrac to assist in the drafting of the treaty by which Charles agreed to cede him the throne of Spain, rode off in the direction of Bayonne.

This treaty was dated 5 May 1808. The Emperor did not wait for Ferdinand's abdication, dated 6 May, by which the Prince renounced his rights to his father 'as a proof of my love, obedience and submission and to accede to the request which Your Majesty has reiterated on several occasions'. 'Animated by the desire to put a rapid term to the anarchy which at the present time is rife in Spain,' began the treaty concluded between Charles and Napoleon. Charles then referred to the 'factions which have divided my family' and ended by ceding his rights to the throne to Napoleon and to the prince whom the Emperor would choose to replace him on the throne of Spain.

Napoleon guaranteed a refuge on French soil to the King, the Queen and her family, and to the Prince of the Peace. They were to receive the Château de Chambord and an annual subsidy of six million francs. While the Château was being prepared for them The Kings and Godoy would take up residence at the Château de Compiègne. But the Emperor was too fond of Chambord to give it up. And as for Compiegne, he wrote:

during their sojourn at Compiègne, the sovereigns are to occupy the rooms reserved for foreign royalty on the pretext that the large apartments are not furnished. In time they will get used to being where they are and then I shall have the use of the palace myself when I want to stay there for big hunting battues. The Prince of the Peace [he added to these instructions] can live wherever he likes. He is of no importance whatsoever.

A further treaty was signed with Ferdinand on 10 May. He was assigned a château in Navarre and a subsidy of four hundred thousand francs a year. An equal sum was to be awarded to his brother Carlos and to his uncle the Infante Don Antonio who had now joined him in Bayonne. They were to be housed temporarily in Talleyrand's Château de Valençay and this is where in fact they spent the seven years of their exile.

Josephine was full of forebodings. Her cartomancer, Mademoiselle Adèle Le Normand, whom even Napoleon had consulted, for he was a superstitious Corsican, had predicted doom for herself and for the Emperor: when Josephine reminded Napoleon of the prediction he only laughed and replied vindictively: 'Talleyrand dared to oppose me. According to him, the conquest of Spain is high treason. Well then, he must participate in it if it be such and he must become the overseer of the Princes at Valençay. That's not giving him a very distinguished role in the play, is it, Josephine?'

'Talleyrand will make a bad enemy,' she replied sadly. 'He is the prince of politicians. He understands the mechanism of the whole machine and directs the motions of the invisible means. He possesses the key to every cabinet in Europe. He has the ear of every minister. He will be able to make you descend from the throne.'

Napoleon flew into a temper. 'By God, Madam, if those are Mademoiselle Normand's predictions, I shall have her arrested. I beg you, Madam, I abjure you, never to speak to me of her again.'

Soon afterwards Monsieur de Talleyrand received a letter from the Emperor giving orders for the Princes' reception. It was planned down to the last detail, like a military campaign.

The Prince of Asturias, his uncle the Infante Don Antonio and his brother the Infante Don Carlos will leave here on Wednesday, spend Friday and Saturday at Bordeaux, and reach Valençay on Tuesday. I want you to be there by Monday evening. My chamberlain Tournon has been posted there to see that everything is ready for their reception. Arrange for the provision of table and bed-linen and all that is needful for the kitchen. They will have eight or ten persons in attendance and as many, or perhaps twice as many, servants. I am ordering the General who is acting as Senior Inspector of the Paris Gendarmerie to organize the police service.

I want these Princes to be received without public ceremonial, but decently and attentively. You must do all you can to keep them amused. If there is a theatre at Valençay and you could arrange for some actors to go there, it would not be a bad idea. Then you could get Madame de Talleyrand to come with four or five other ladies. If the Prince of Asturias were to form an attachment to some good-looking woman whom one could depend upon, so much the better: it would give us an additional means of watching him, and I am particularly anxious that he should commit no political indiscretions; that is why I want him to be occupied and amused. If I were vindictive, I should shut him up in a fortress. But as he has thrown himself upon my mercy and promised to do nothing without my instructions, and as everything in Spain is going well, I have decided to send him to this country place and to surround him with pleasures and spies. Your own part in the business is honourable enough. To entertain and amuse these illustrious young personages is thoroughly in character with your station and with your rank. Eight or ten days spent in their company will acquaint you with their thoughts and help me to decide what I should do.

Monsieur de Talleyrand's opinion about the Emperor's role in the Spanish trap was summed up to his face a little later in the year when they met at Nantes. 'If a gentleman commits follies, if he keeps mistresses, treats his wife badly, is guilty of serious injustices towards his friends, he will be blamed no doubt; but if he is rich, powerful and intelligent, society will treat him with indulgence. But if that man cheats at cards, he will immediately be banished from decent society and never forgiven. Sire, you have sealed your fate at Bayonne. You have committed the unforgivable crime: you have cheated at cards.'

It must be admitted that Napoleon's captives bore him no grudge. Every one of them bade friendly adieux to their captor before they rolled off in their respective carriages to their different destinations and destinies. They were friendlier to Napoleon than to their own kith and kin. The Kings and Ferdinand never embraced, never met, never saw each other again.

After they had left Bayonne, Napoleon prepared to meet his brother Joseph and the Spanish Cortes which he had convened on French soil. 'Our very beloved brother Joseph,' he declared in an imperial decree, 'will put an end to the interreign for the good of Spain.' Murat took his place as King of Naples.

'Everything is satisfactorily ended at Bayonne,' Napoleon wrote jubilantly to General Bessières.

Josephine was pleased to see him in such a good mood. He seemed to have recaptured some of the gaiety of their early married life. The scent of spring was intoxicating. The hawthorn was in bloom, the hedgerows a mosaic of wild flowers. One afternoon the Emperor took Josephine for a drive along the coast. Suddenly he ordered the coachman to stop, seized his wife by the hand and cried: 'Come on, let's go and paddle!'

They ran down to the beach hand in hand, laughing like children. After they had paddled for a few minutes, Napoleon turned, raced back to the beach, picked up Josephine's shoes and went off with them to the coach so that she had to rejoin it barefoot. Josephine was radiant. Perhaps this prank was a good omen? It seemed to prove that Napoleon was still fond of her, that he would not divorce her as Fouché had warned? She was wrong. It was only a passing mood . . .

'This is the last act of the comedy,' Napoleon had written prematurely to Monsieur de Talleyrand. True enough. But the first act of the drama of his downfall was about to begin. Stormclouds were gathering over Spain. Juntas sprang up spontaneously in every province against the French occupation and that of Cadiz appealed to England for help. What the Emperor had once foreseen and feared was coming to pass: Spain and England joined forces. On 4 July 1808 George III solemnly announced to Parliament in London: 'I view with the liveliest interest the loyal and determined spirit manifested in resisting the violence and perfidy with which the dearest rights of the Spanish nation have been assailed. The Kingdom thus nobly struggling against the usurpation and tyranny of France can no longer be considered as the enemy of Great Britain, but is recognized by me as a natural friend and ally.'

Goya, the court painter of the Bourbons, who had mocked his royal patrons to their doltish faces, took up his burin and wielded it like a sword to portray the sufferings of his countrymen in his famous series of etchings, 'The Disasters of War'. The Peninsular War.

EPILOGUE

So the curtain falls on the tragi-comedy of Bayonne and Napoleon's Spanish trap. But what happened to the main characters? How did they react to their circumstances? How long did they live?

Ferdinand enjoyed himself at Valençay. He had never been so free. In Madrid and the other royal palaces he and his brothers were never allowed to walk in the gardens without a written permission from the King, so it was a novelty for them to be able to ride and hunt freely, and to dance. Ferdinand was never allowed to dance in Spain.

Monsieur de Talleyrand had a fine library but the Prince did not spend much time in it. He was not bookish.

People blamed him because he wrote to Napoleon during his exile in laudatory terms. To which the Prince would no doubt have replied: 'Why not? Napoleon was a great man and he paid me a handsome pension. Not always on the dot, and not as much as had been stipulated in our treaty, but I depended on him entirely for a living.'

The Prince spent seven years in Valençay before returning to Spain as King Ferdinand VII in 1814. He had had no experience of government or politics and he had inherited his mother's character. He suppressed the Liberal constitution, restored the Inquisition and revoked the Salic Law so that his daughter Isabel could reign after him. His brother Charles refused to recognize her and this was the cause of the Carlist wars. Ferdinand married three times during his reign and died in 1833. Nobody regretted his death.

Some of his friends, for example the Duke of Infantado, went over to the French side and served under Joseph. Canon Escoiquiz eventually became one of Ferdinand's ministers but he was too interfering and ambitious so he was dismissed. He died in Andalusia.

Ferdinand's sister Luisetta ended her life as Duchess of Lucca, in 1824. She was always pestering her brother for money. He refused to allow her to receive Godoy at Lucca as she had wanted to. In the end she agreed that he 'was a monster' but maybe that was because she wanted to wheedle a loan out of her brother at the time she wrote that letter with its antagonistic references to the ex-favourite.

Charles IV died in Rome in 1819, shortly after the death of Maria Luisa. He was on a visit and was not present at her deathbed but faithful Manuel was with her till the end.

Maria Luisa, in a will drawn up in 1817, had made Manuel Godoy her sole legatee. The will was anulled. Manuel returned it to Ferdinand himself. It would of course have been contested.

Ferdinand continued to persecute Godoy after The Kings' deaths. He had his lands and effects confiscated. His last years were spent in Paris where he could be seen many a morning in the Tuileries gardens feeding the birds and playing with children. His own children and his wife, Pepita Tudó (whom he had married in 1828), deserted him. He felt this more keenly than the change in his position. So he confided to Lord Holland who paid him a visit in 1838, fourteen years before Godoy's death in 1852. (He outlived The Kings and Ferdinand.)

Lord Holland suggested to Godoy that he could have made

a fortune from his memoirs if he had included more personal anecdotes and accounts of palace life. By that he meant salacious details about his 'enigmatic relationship' – as he had referred to it years earlier – with the Queen. But Godoy was a Spanish hidalgo. He never revealed his private life.

Lord Holland also invited Godoy to live in England but he graciously declined. He could not forget that if it had not been for Napoleon's desire to ruin England he would never have ruined Spain and their paths would not have crossed. And besides, France was less alien to a Spaniard than England.

Godoy could never bring himself to return to Spain even after Ferdinand's death. It would have been pleasant to drive through the Prado, he remarked to Lord Holland wistfully, but on the other hand it would also have conjured up poignant memories, so he thought it would be better to stay where he was – in his little flat in the rue de la Michaudière. Queen Isabel II granted him a small pension. He was buried in Pére Lachaise . . .

Godoy would have been nothing without Charles and particularly Maria Luisa. Nobody can deny his loyalty to The Kings, whatever other shortcomings he may be blamed for. True, he was over-ambitious in his young days, vain and unscrupulous. In another age and other circumstances he might have got by without causing disgrace to his country but he was no match for Napoleon and his ambitions.

At the end of his life at St Helena Napoleon admitted that he had 'embarked badly on the Spanish affair. The immorality of it was too patent, the injustice too cynical and the whole thing wears an ugly look since I have fallen; for the attempt is only seen in its hideous nakedness, deprived of all majesty and of the many benefits which would have resulted from my original plan.'

Since Napoleon set his Spanish mousetrap the world has lived through so many more iniquitous usurpations and occupations that we are prepared – as the present author is – to take a slightly more lenient view of the adventure. Look at Goya's portraits of the Spanish court. Consider how those puppets behaved; consider their total lack of interest in their people's welfare, their personal futility and the impoverished state of Spain when Napoleon turned to that country for assistance. Was it not a temptation for a man of his calibre to treat the Spanish Bourbons and their favourite with contempt? Was he not very patient with them for eight long years, before his final coup?

These considerations do not entirely exonerate him, but it must be admitted that 'the Trinity' and Ferdinand were enough to try the temper of a less impetuous foe. From 1800 to 1808 Napoleon waged a personal battle with the Spanish court; during that period he dealt only with mice. His mistake was to ignore what lay outside the trap he laid for them: the people of Spain. They were not mice; they were lions: untamed and untameable.

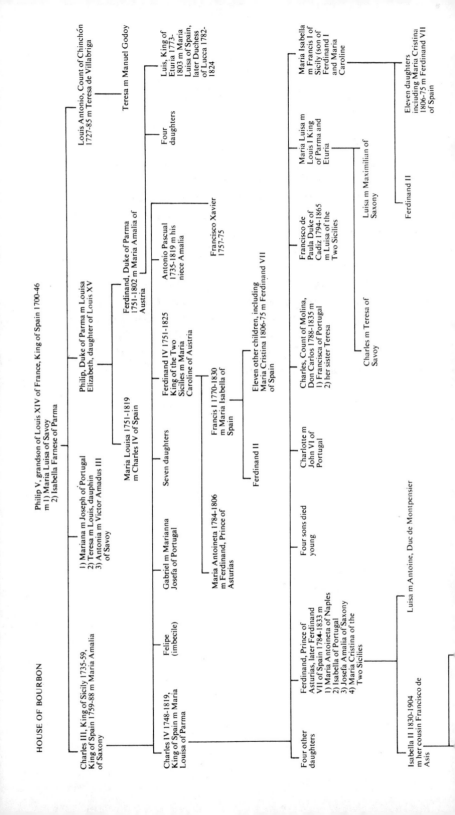

HOUSE OF BOURBON

SELECT BIBLIOGRAPHY

Most memoir sources, used principally for dialogue, have
been discreetly referred to in the course of my book, so as
not to interrupt the flow of what purports to be a well
documented story but not a learned tome for scholars, who
should know the sources better than I do. I append the
following short list for readers who would like to pursue the
subject further.

Mémoires de Monsieur Charles Alquier, Paris, 1887
Gomez de Arteche, *El Reinado de Carlos IV* (3 vols.),
Madrid, 1897
Miguel Artola (ed.), *Memorias de los Tiempos de Fernando
VII*, Madrid, 1957
Duchesse D'Abrantès, *Souvenirs d'une Ambassade et d'un
séjour en Espagne et au Portugal,* Brussels, 1828
Martin Armstrong, *Spanish Circus,* London, 1937
Harold Acton, *The Bourbons of Naples,* London, 1950
C. Baratech, *Revolución y Reacción en el reinado de Carlos
IV,* Madrid, 1957
L.F.J. de Bausset, *Mémoires Anecdotiques de l'interieur du
Palais Imperial*, Paris, 1827
Raymond Carr, *Spain,* London, 1966
Jacques Chastenet, *Godoy, Master of Spain,* London, 1950
Jean-François Chabrun, *Goya,* London, 1965
Juan de Escoiquiz, *Memorias*, Madrid, 1915
André Fugier, *Napoléon et l'Espagne*, Paris, 1930
Hans Roger Madol, *Godoy,* London, 1934
Andrès Muriel, *Historia de Carlos IV*, Madrid, 1959
Manuel Godoy, *Memoirs* (4 vols.), Paris, 1836
Peréz de Guzmán (ed.), *Cartas Confidenciales de la Reina
Maria Luisa y de Manuel Godoy*, Madrid, 1935
Peréz de Guzmán, *Estudios de la vida, reinado, proscripción y
muerte de Carlos IV y de Maria Luisa*, Madrid, 1908

Carlos Seco Serrano, *Historia de Carlos IV*, Madrid, 1955

Louis Madelin, *The Consulate and the Empire,* London, 1934

Geoffroi de Grandmaison, *L'Espagne et Napoléon,* Paris, 1935

Comte Murat, *Murat, Lieutenant General de l'Empereur*, Paris, 1867

Duc de Broglie (ed.), *Memoirs of the Prince of Talleyrand,* London, 1891

Jean Orieux, *Talleyrand*, Paris, 1970

Napoleon's *Letters* (various editions)

Sir Charles Petrie, *The Spanish Royal House*, London, 1950

Adèle le Normand, *The History and Secret Memoirs of the Empress Josephine,* London, 1825

Manuel Izquierdo Hernandez, *Antecedentes y Comienzos del Reinado de Fernando VII*, Madrid, 1963

Prince Sixte de Bourbon, *La Reine d'Etrie*, Paris, 1928

General Savary (Duc de Rovigo), *Memoirs* (4 vols.), Paris, 1828

The Spanish Journal of Lady Elizabeth Holland, London, 1910

Lord Holland, *Foreign Reminiscences,* London, 1850

Antonina Vallentin, *This I Saw: Life and Times of Goya,* London, 1956

Abbé de Pradt, *Mémoires Historiques sur la Révolution d'Espagne,* Paris, 1816

Angel Salcedo Ruiz, *La Epoca de Goya*, Madrid, n.d.

Georges Roux, *Napoléon et le Guêpier Espagnol,* Paris, 1970